GLORY

WHEN HEAVEN
INVADES EARTH

B O B   S O R G E

gain a renewed vision for the highest goal of worship

Other books by Bob Sorge:
- *SECRETS OF THE SECRET PLACE*
- *DEALING WITH THE REJECTION AND PRAISE OF MAN*
- *PAIN, PERPLEXITY, AND PROMOTION: A prophetic interpretation of the book of Job*
- *THE FIRE OF GOD'S LOVE*
- *THE FIRE OF DELAYED ANSWERS*
- *IN HIS FACE: A prophetic call to renewed focus*
- *EXPLORING WORSHIP: A practical guide to praise and worship*
- *Exploring Worship WORKBOOK & DISCUSSION GUIDE*

GLORY: When Heaven Invades Earth
Copyright (c) 2000 by Bob Sorge
Published by Oasis House
P.O. Box 127
Greenwood, Missouri 64034-0127

www.oasishouse.net

Edited by Edie Veach.

Printed in the United States of America
Library of Congress Catalog Card Number: 00-092747
International Standard Book Number: 0-9621185-9-1

Contents

Glory: Destination Planet Earth

*H*urtling through space and careening through the blackness in ominous silence...rolling and churning as it races toward sudden impact...carrying enough explosive power within the sheer weight of its immensity that—when it hits Earth—it will trigger cataclysmic shock waves that could wipe out mankind and bury our globe in another ice age. Such is the foreboding specter of a gigantic meteor or comet heading for planet Earth.

Could there be such a destructive heavenly body out there in the darkness of space right now, headed inevitably toward our planet? Only God knows.

Scientists have surmised that meteors have hit and drastically affected our planet's history. Even if it's thousands of years away, the possibility of yet another collision with a foreign heavenly body is very real.

Whether a meteor is heading our way I do not know; but I do know of something else that is scheduled to intercept earth's orbiting trajectory. It's out there somewhere, moving toward our planet at the speed of light. When it explodes into our domain, it will change everything that we have come to know about our reality.

I don't know when it's due to arrive. All I know is that it is most certainly coming, and the Bible describes its coming with words such as "quickly," "suddenly," and "soon." What is this heavenly entity heading our way? In one word, it's Glory. This planet is on an unstoppable, inexorable, irreversible crash course with the Glory of God.

ON CANAAN'S THRESHOLD

God prophesied our collision with His Glory, and the context of His first declaration of that fact is very fascinating. It came at the time when the children of Israel had made the trek from Sinai to Canaan's border, and they sent twelve men into Canaan to spy out the land and bring back a report. Two of the spies (Caleb and Joshua) brought a good report to the people, saying, " 'Let us go up at once and take possession, for we are well able to overcome it' " (Number 13:30).

> *This planet is on an unstoppable,*
> *inexorable, irreversible crash course*
> *with the Glory of God.*

The other ten brought an evil report, saying, " 'We are not able to go up against the people, for they are stronger than we. The land through which we have gone as spies is a land that devours its inhabitants, and all the people whom we saw in it are men of great stature. There we saw the giants; and we were like grasshoppers in our own sight, and so we were in their sight' " (Numbers 13:31-33).

In response to this bad news, the entire congregation lifted their voices and wept. They complained about Moses and Aaron, about God Himself, and then they spoke of selecting a leader and returning to Egypt.

When Joshua and Caleb tried to talk some sense into the people, the entire congregation said to stone them with stones. It was at that point "the glory of the LORD appeared in the tabernacle of meeting before all the children of Israel" (Numbers 14:10). We know from other passages that the appearance of God's Glory was like a cloud. On this occasion, the Glory of the Lord appeared to the people, not as a token of blessing and favor, but as a harbinger of imminent anger. In other words, this appearance of Glory was a massive "early warning system" signaling the people that trouble was brewing for them.

GOD'S HOLY INDIGNATION

God was so angry that He said to Moses, " 'I will strike them with the pestilence and disinherit them, and I will make of you a nation greater and mightier than they' " (Numbers 14;12). God was willing to scrap over 500 years worth of investment in Abraham's lineage and start all over with Moses. This was a firm offer. God was saying, "Moses, I'll make you the head of the nation instead of Abraham, and I'll do a better job with your descendants than I did with his." Here's why God was so steamed. He had shown them His Glory, but they still didn't believe. He said, " 'How long will they not believe Me, with all the signs which I have performed among them?' " (Number 14:11).

God's plan was simple:

"First, I will show My Glory *to* you."

"Then, I will show My Glory *through* you to the nation."

But the people said no. When it was time for God's Glory to be manifested through them to the earth, they refused. Even though God's Glory had come *to* them, they couldn't believe it could be manifest *through* them. Sounds familiar, doesn't it? God's Glory can come to us, but we have difficulty believing it could be manifested through us. So in His anger at their unbelief, God talked of destroying them all.

Moses stepped in quickly and began to intercede for the people. Moses told the Lord that if He disposed of the people, He would get a bad reputation among the heathen. Moses prayed, "Now if You kill these people as one man, then the nations which have heard of Your fame will speak, saying, 'Because the LORD was not able to bring this people to the land which He swore to give them, therefore He killed them in the wilderness' " (Number 14:15-16). Moses asked the Lord to be merciful and forgive the people.

GOD'S VOW

Now look at God's response: "Then the LORD said: 'I have pardoned, according to your word; but truly, as I live, all the earth shall be filled with the glory of the LORD" (Numbers 14:20-21). In other words God was saying, "Okay, Moses, I'll forgive them this time. But truly,"—and now He's going to confirm His words with an oath. For the first time in Scripture, He invokes the oath, "as I live." "As I live all the earth shall be filled with the glory of the LORD." God is underscoring His rock-hard resolve in the matter. Absolutely nothing will dissuade or soften God's determination.

In other words, God is saying, "If these people don't want to be conduits of My Glory, well okay, I forgive them. But make no mistake, Moses. *It will happen!* My Glory is going to come to earth; I swear it. And not only is it going to come, it is going to *fill* the entire earth!" Ladies and gentlemen, God's Glory is coming! It is an inevitable reality that is going to inundate planet earth. We cannot avoid it or run from it. Glory is coming!

> *God's Glory is coming!*
> *It is an inevitable reality that is*
> *going to inundate planet earth.*

God cannot be talked out of the resolve of His heart. Forever this certainty is settled in heaven. God is irrevocably determined to saturate the entire earth with His Glory. Ready or not, it's coming. Promise.

A BRIEF OVERVIEW

What is the Glory of God?
What will it look like when it comes?
How can we prepare for it?
Is it possible to hinder or help the coming Glory?
These are the issues we will address in the coming pages. We have been created with a deep hunger for Glory. The human spirit, made alive by the Spirit of God, pants for the fullness of

God's Glory in the here and now. I hope to validate and fuel that desire. My prayer is that through the insights the Lord has burned into my heart you might be freshly awakened to the beauty of Christ's face, and be filled with the assurance of His certain visitation to your life, church, and circle of influence. May His Glory come—to you!

2

Defining Glory

"Glory" as the term is used in Scripture is a somewhat elusive term to define succinctly. So the first obvious question is, "What do you mean by Glory? What is the Glory of God?" That's an important question that needs to be answered before we move forward any further.

Glory is by nature a rather vague, ethereal concept that many struggle to comprehend clearly. The task of defining Glory is exacerbated by the fact that it is used in a variety of ways in Scripture. Before explaining what I mean by Glory, I want to distinguish what I *don't* mean in my usage of the word.

This brief book can hardly begin to exhaust the vastness of the subject of God's Glory, so we are focusing on only one aspect of Glory. In this chapter, I would like to survey the various ways that Glory is used in the Scriptures and, then, pinpoint the precise application of Glory to which this book is dedicated.

First let's look at the various uses of "Glory" in the Bible that are not covered in this book. At the end of the chapter will come the definition of Glory that we will pursue. So here it is, the various usages of "Glory" in the Bible. (Note: the definitions used in this chapter are the author's.)

GLORY AS A VERB

When "glory" appears as a verb, its meaning is quite different from its occurrences as a noun. (For the purposes of this book, I am capitalizing "Glory" as a noun but not "glory" as a verb.) The verb "to glory" carries two general meanings in its usage in Scripture.

1. To glory: "to delight in"

We are enjoined by Scripture, "Glory in His holy name" (Psalm 105:3). In this and similar instances, the word "glory" means "to delight in, to revel in, to take pleasure in." In this sense of the word a parent might be said to glory in his or her children while they play. Family members will enjoy and delight in each other while they watch them being themselves. In a similar way, when we glory in God's holy name we are enjoying and delighting in Him.

2. To glory: "to boast in" or "to take pride in"

When I think of glorying in the sense of boasting or taking pride in something, I envision the proud celebrations of a sports team that has just won a significant tournament. It could be said that the team glories in its victory. This meaning of the word "glory" is found in many verses, but I will quote just two here:

- But "he who glories, let him glory in the LORD" (2 Corinthians 10:17).
- Thus says the LORD: "Let not the wise man glory in his wisdom, let not the mighty man glory in his might, nor let the rich man glory in his riches; but let him who glories glory in this, that he understands and knows Me" (Jeremiah 9:23).

These verses declare that our only boast is that we know God. We glory (boast) in God.

These are the two general meanings of "glory" as a verb, and while "glory" appears as a verb many times in Scripture, we are not studying these in this book. Now let's look at the noun, "Glory."

GLORY AS A NOUN

I see Glory used, as a noun, in four distinct ways in Scripture. We will look only briefly at the first three, and then devote the rest of this book to the fourth dynamic of Glory.

1.   Glory: "Honor, reputation, dignity, praise."

Glory is used to describe the dignity and honor of both man and God. There is a Glory of man, and there is a Glory of God. Here are a few examples to illustrate this usage in Scripture.

   a.   The Glory of man:
   •   Awake, my glory! Awake, lute and harp! I will awaken the dawn (Psalm 57:8).
   (David is calling for the dignity/honor given him by God to be aroused, in order that he might give Glory to God with the Glory with which he himself was crowned.)
   •   For You have made him [man] a little lower than the angels, and You have crowned him with glory and honor (Psalm 8:5).
   (By creating man in His image, God invested in man a profound dimension of dignity that far surpasses that of any other creation on earth.)

   b.   The Glory of God: (this is one of the most common usages of "Glory" in the Bible, referring to the honor and praise and reputation of God Himself)
   •   I am the LORD, that is My name; and My glory I will not give to another, nor My praise to carved images (Isaiah 42:8).
   (God will not share the honor and renown of His name with anyone or anything else.)
   •   Give to the LORD, O families of the peoples, give to

the LORD glory and strength (1 Chronicles 16:28).
(To give God Glory here means to give Him praise
and honor for the excellence of His being.)

- And one cried to another and said: "Holy, holy, holy
is the LORD of hosts; the whole earth is full of His
glory!" (Isaiah 6:3).
(The earth is full of natural beauty which declares
the honor and praise of God without cessation.
There is an important distinction to make here, because the earth is full of God's Glory in terms of
honor and praise to Him; but the earth is *not* yet full
of God's Glory in the way we will be defining it
under point 4 below.)

2. Glory: "Endowment of blessing, power, and life."

In some instances, "Glory" is used to describe the awesome
power of God. In accordance with this second meaning of Glory,
I will point to two verses where Glory is used to speak of God's
infilling power. In fact, "Glory" could almost be translated
"Power" in these verses because of how it is used.

- Then your light shall break forth like the morning, your
healing shall spring forth speedily, and your righteous-
ness shall go before you; the glory of the LORD shall be
your rear guard (Isaiah 58:8).
(The Glory of God is described as a power which will
protect God's people.)
- "And the glory which You gave Me I have given them,
that they may be one just as We are one" (John 17:22).
(Jesus said He has given His Glory to us as an enabling
power that will produce true unity among believers.)

3. Glory: "The heavenly dimension where the magnitude of
God's personhood irradiates throughout the heavenlies."

In this third usage of Glory, its meaning is virtually inter-
changeable with our word "heaven." God's people are destined
for Glory—that is, heaven. Heaven is a place of Glory. The

Glory of heaven derives from the very person of God Himself. Just as our sun radiates energy and light, God exudes Glory. God is such a dynamically blazing inferno that the radiation of His person is called Glory. Glory imbues and sustains all of heaven. It is the air of heaven. The reality of God's Glory in the heavenlies is more real than the seat you're sitting in right now. His Glory is the ultimate reality. It is the tangible manifestation of the infinite beauty and splendor of His magnificent face.

Following are three portions (among many) that refer to this Glory:

- You will guide me with Your counsel, and afterward receive me to glory [heaven] (Psalm 73:24).
- Like the appearance of a rainbow in a cloud on a rainy day, so was the appearance of the brightness all around it. This was the appearance of the likeness of the glory [heavenlies] of the LORD. So when I saw it, I fell on my face, and I heard a voice of One speaking (Ezekiel 1:28).
- And without controversy great is the mystery of godliness: God was manifested in the flesh, justified in the Spirit, seen by angels, preached among the Gentiles, believed on in the world, received up in glory [heaven] (1 Timothy 3:16).

And now to the fourth scriptural usage of Glory as a noun.

4. Glory: "The invasion of God's reality into the human sphere."

This final distinctive of Glory is the sphere of this book. "Glory" is used in the Bible, in this final sense, to describe the action of God whereby He takes of His Glory which is eternally existent in heaven, pushes through the veil that separates natural and spiritual realities, and reveals within the parameters of our time and space the splendor of His magnificent beauty and splendor.

> *"Glory" is used in the Bible, in this final sense, to describe the action of God whereby He takes of His Glory which is eternally existent in heaven, pushes through the veil that separates natural and spiritual realities, and reveals within the parameters of our time and space the splendor of His magnificent beauty and splendor.*

There is coming a time when the Glory of the heavenlies is going to invade our natural plane, and mankind is going to be abruptly awakened to the might and power of God's Presence. It is to this revelation of Glory which the following verses point.

- For the earth will be filled with the knowledge of the glory of the LORD, as the waters cover the sea (Habakkuk 2:14).
- "And I will shake all nations, and they shall come to the Desire of All Nations, and I will fill this temple with glory," says the LORD of hosts (Haggai 2:7).
- The glory of the LORD shall be revealed, and all flesh shall see it together; for the mouth of the LORD has spoken (Isaiah 40:5).

Come with me now as we look at this final aspect of Glory—the invasion of God's reality into the human sphere.

Preparing For Glory

God's Glory is about to invade our planet. And the truth is, we're not altogether ready for Glory. We have no idea what will happen when it comes, so we don't realize how unprepared we really are.

But God is committed to preparing us for Glory. The people were not ready for God's Glory when Jesus came two thousand years ago, so God sent John the Baptist ahead of Christ's face to prepare the way. In a similar way, He has promised to send Elijah once again in order to prepare the endtime generation for the final great outpouring of Glory (Mark 9:12).

Isaiah described John's ministry by showing how he would prepare the people. These same truths apply to us today as we seek to prepare our hearts for God's Glory.

> *"The voice of one crying in the wilderness: 'Prepare the way of the LORD; make straight in the desert a highway for our God. Every valley shall be exalted and every mountain and hill brought low; the crooked places shall be made straight and the rough places smooth; the glory of the LORD shall be revealed, and all flesh shall see it together; for the mouth of the LORD has spoken' "* (Isaiah 40:3-5).

This passage describes how God prepares His people for Glory. He builds a highway in the hearts of His people by filling in the valleys, bringing down the high places, making the crooked places straight, and the rough places smooth. These are all operations of God upon the human heart, preparing us for His visitation. Let's look at each phrase individually.

"THE VOICE OF ONE CRYING IN THE WILDERNESS"

God took John into the wilderness to nurture his voice (his message). The principle remains true: You have to go to the wilderness to get a voice. Some who desire to gain a voice may go to theological seminary, but that's not where you get a voice. Seminaries produce echoes (those who can echo the many voices from which they've gleaned). John the Baptist had to go to the wilderness to get his voice. To produce a voice requires the solitude and forsakenness of the wilderness.

God will be leading some of His servants into the wilderness in this hour to equip them with a voice for this generation. He will give them a message that will help the church prepare for Glory. They will be mouthpieces of God's heart to His endtime bride.

It can sound a bit sensational—to be a voice with a message that prepares God's people for Glory. But to garner that voice will require an unusual degree of consecration to God's purposes as He takes you through the wilderness.

A wilderness is by definition a place where few people dwell, primarily because conditions are not conducive to the everyday lifestyles of most people. Thus, it is a place of aloneness, of imposed confinement, of personal inconvenience, of social ostracization, of unfriendly surroundings. It is the place where God meets with His man or His woman. It's the one-on-one meeting ground of profound spiritual formation. This is where God gives a man a message that is formed from his life rather than his library.

John the Baptist had no mentor. Nor did Elijah. Nor did Job nor Abraham nor Jacob nor Joseph nor Moses nor Naomi nor David nor Paul for that matter. You must do the wilderness by yourself. It's the voice of "one." Nobody else but you and God.

God designs the wilderness in such a way that nobody can mentor you through it. Nobody else has answers for the unique dryness of your desert. You're on your own. Those who are given a voice to a generation do not find their message through a mentoring relationship, but rather in the solitude of the wilderness.

To give you a voice, God must first snuff out all the other voices. There is a time for study and reading and gleaning from the many voices, but then the time comes when the books are put away and a man (or a woman) meets alone with his God. He begins to be shaped by nothing but the Word and the Spirit.

And the journey is long and arduous. That's why it says the voice of one "crying." A cry is an expression of pain. The loneliness itself is one of the sources of pain. It's through the crucible of the wilderness, with its attending tears, that a cry is birthed deep in the heart that no amount of resistance or distress can snuff out. The intimidation of Pharisees cannot silence these lips. Although this voice will be controversial, the cry will compel men to stop and listen. The message will be a call to repentance that prepares the way for the Glory of God.

What does the voice say?

> *It's through the crucible of the wilderness, with its attending tears, that a cry is birthed deep in the heart that no amount of resistance or distress can snuff out.*

"'PREPARE THE WAY OF THE LORD'"

The voice cries, "Get ready—the Lord of Glory is coming!" So what must we do to get ready? One of the first things on God's heart is that we come to know "the way of the Lord."

God is always self-consistent and true to His way. He works only through man, but He demands things be done His way. Those who try to do kingdom business their own way will soon discover that God is no longer doing business with them. God refuses to act unilaterally without man, for that would violate

His intention for man's participation. However, He waits to work alongside man until man conforms to His way.

Since His ways are a universe above our ways (Isaiah 55:9), God must exert great energy to get us to align with His ways. Hence, the wilderness. The wilderness is God's method of awakening us to the beauty and wonder of His ways. God took John the Baptist into the wilderness, not only to give him a voice, but also to conform his ways to God's ways so that the message would not be compromised by the iniquities (hidden shortcomings) of the messenger.

When those with a forerunner message emerge in God's time from the wilderness they will help God's people to align with God's ways, and they will foretell the coming of God's Glory.

"'MAKE STRAIGHT IN THE DESERT A HIGHWAY FOR OUR GOD'"

God likes to travel in the desert (see Song of Solomon 3). It's in the desert that human hindrances to His purposes are starved out. With that statement I am referring in part to the human devices that naturally attach to the operations of the kingdom when times are good. Devices that seemed adequate in better times are found to be powerless in the dry seasons. The driest times cause our human mechanisms to shrivel and die, and thus the desert becomes the greatest conduit for God's visitation.

The Hebrew word for "make straight" in the phrase above means, "To be straight, right, upright, pleasing, good." The same word *(yashar)* is translated as the English word "direct" in Proverbs 3:5-6, "Trust in the LORD with all your heart, and lean not on your own understanding; in all your ways acknowledge Him, and He shall *direct* [make straight] your paths." In other words, God will "straighten out" the path of His devoted servants who trust in Him.

The enemy is constantly seeking to twist the straight ways of the Lord in an attempt to hinder Glory's free flow. On one occasion Elymas, a sorcerer, tried to hinder the kingdom's advance by twisting the truth. That's why Paul said to Elymas, "'You son of the devil...will you not cease perverting the straight ways of the Lord?'" (Acts 13:10).

It is very important to God that His servants represent His ways accurately to others, and that they can discern when His ways are being violated. It's possible to utter right words in a wrong way so that God's ways are misrepresented. God jealously yearns for His passionate heart for mankind to be accurately conveyed to the peoples. We must speak properly of His ways if we desire to be visited by His Glory. Let me share an incident that makes this truth personal for me.

For years I have struggled with a long-term physical affliction, seeking the Lord fervently for healing, and on one occasion someone said to me, "Bob, even if you're never healed in this life, this affliction will have been worth it because of what it has produced in you." When I prayed about that statement I thought of the words, "Do not pervert the straight ways of the Lord." Because the straight ways of God are this: He wounds, but then He binds up; He kills, but He then makes alive; He imprisons, but then He liberates His captives. So I am committed to declaring the straight ways of the Lord because I am desperate for a visitation of His Glory. The straight way of the Lord is this: Not only has God changed me profoundly in this crucible of affliction, but He is also going to deliver me in His time and way. When God imprisons one of His servants in a furnace of affliction for the purpose of character formation, His highest purpose is to release that prisoner in the fullness of time into deliverance, freedom, and increased fruitfulness.

If God has brought you into the desert, His heart intention for your desert is that a highway of holiness might be built in your heart upon which He can ride as He comes to you with deliverance power. I am convinced that this is the straight way of the Lord. And to whatever degree my understanding of His way is wrong, I fervently desire for the Lord to straighten out every crooked thing that remains in my heart and understanding.

"'EVERY VALLEY SHALL BE EXALTED'"

To prepare us for Glory, God first of all fills in the valleys of our lives. This refers to the low places in our hearts that need to be filled with confidence in God.

It is absolutely exhilarating when the Holy Spirit rushes to fill in our inadequacies, insecurities, and weaknesses. "I can't" becomes "I can do all things through Christ who strengthens me." Unbelief can no longer be a canyon within us, swallowing up the blessed future of God's chosen ones. The valley of unbelief must submit to the infilling of faith through the power of the Holy Spirit. God is for us!

I am greatly challenged about Scripture's testimony of Abraham, that "he did not consider his own body, already dead" (Romans 4:19). Although his body was reproductively dead (as was Sarah's), he did not consider his body. He believed God would fulfill His promise of a son, counting God able to fulfill His promise. I have taken this as personal encouragement to say to the Lord, "Lord, I will do anything You call me to do. Even if my body is seemingly incapable of doing it, I will not consider my body. I will not consider my incapabiltiies, liabilities, and disabilities. I will obey Your word!"

> *"Lord, I will do anything You call me to do. Even if my body is seemingly incapable of doing it, I will not consider my body. I will not consider my incapabiltiies, liabilities, and disabilities. I will obey Your word!"*

"Every valley" also refers to those things which are despised in the sight of men, especially by those in religious establishments. God seems to delight in bringing His Glory through means that are disdained by religious systems. He comes to the things that are weak and despised and dignifies them with His Glory.

Before Glory comes, the church will have to elevate those things that are despised by the world, such as modesty, chastity, inner beauty, self-effacement, willingness to serve, and willingness to be in the background. These are the kinds of values the Holy Spirit is exalting in this hour.

"'AND EVERY MOUNTAIN AND HILL BROUGHT LOW"

Nothing is more glorious than when God fills in the valleys—and nothing is more painful than when God levels the mountains. "Every mountain" refers to the high things in our lives against which God sets His face, such as pride, private agendas, personal ambitions, self-promotion, self-reliance, self-determination, rebellion, competitiveness, etc. God is setting His face against flowery orations, hype, and personality-driven leadership styles that get God's people enamored with the messenger instead of the Sender.

One of the most painful revelations I received was when God showed me how I as a pastor had made decisions out of a self-seeking desire to build my own ministry. I thought my motives were pure, but God put enough fire on my life to reveal private agendas within my heart that I didn't even know existed. Suddenly I saw how that an insidious desire to grow a powerful ministry had caused me to function out of a spirit of ambition and competitiveness toward the other Gospel-preaching churches of our community. Even though that ambitious element was only a tiny fraction of a mostly pure motivation, it still remains true that a tiny bit of yeast leavens the entire batch of dough. The tiniest particle of ambition can discolor an entire ministry. God targeted this disastrous motivation in my heart by first of all showing it to me, and then secondly by having me confess it verbally to the pastors of my community. Asking those pastors to pray for me played a significant role in bulldozing that mountain of pride into a plane.

"Every mountain" can also refer to prominent ministries which are esteemed by man but which God will bring down because of their faulty foundations. God is disciplining ministries that are operating out of human creativity and talent-driven initiative rather than submissive obedience to the voice of the Spirit.

"Every mountain" may even refer to demonic strongholds, sociological mindsets, and natural hindrances which would stand in opposition to the advance of our glorious Gospel. Every high thing that exalts itself against the knowledge of Christ must be brought down so that God's Glory might visit this planet.

"THE CROOKED PLACES SHALL BE MADE STRAIGHT"

The crooked places are areas in our understanding and ways of operating that we *think* are straight, but before God they are not. John addressed this syndrome when he described the Pharisees and religious leaders of his day as a "brood of vipers" (offspring of venomous snakes). Snakes think they're heading straight toward their target, but in fact they are going crookedly the entire time. It's impossible for a viper to go straight; its pathway is inherently crooked.

By calling the people "vipers," John was trying to straighten the crooked places. The people had been trained by vipers to walk a crooked path. "Then he said to the multitudes that came out to be baptized by him, 'Brood of vipers! Who warned you to flee from the wrath to come?'" (Luke 3:7).

Vipers flee from fire. That's why Paul got bit by the viper when he tried to put the wood in the fire (see Acts 28:3). John came with a message of fire, and the vipers scurried. In a sense, John also got bitten by vipers, a bite which led unto his death. This is the cost sometimes of being a forerunner. It can be dangerous to tackle the crooked places.

"The crooked places" can also refer to sinful secrets we are harboring that no one else but God sees. I am thinking of areas of moral compromise, including unethical money dealings and slightly dishonest income tax returns. It may be hidden for a while, but the time will come when God will say, "No more." And He will expose the crooked places. Either we must deal privately with the crooked places in our hearts, or God will deal with them publicly. Either way, it is essential that we make the crooked places straight if we want a visitation from God.

"'AND THE ROUGH PLACES SMOOTH'"

First of all, this is a reference to personality and character attributes abrasive and counterproductive to the kingdom. All of us have "rough areas" in our lives we are helpless to change in our own strength. Some examples might be ego, anger, argumentativeness, and self-justification. We can't repent of these things until God shows them to us. We are totally dependent upon the Lord to help us smooth out the rough areas of our lives. As He tests us with His refining fire, it is absolutely essential how we respond to His dealings if we are to see His Glory.

This is one reason God adamantly insists we relate closely and vitally to the body of Christ. When we come into contact with others in the church, and their lives are thrown against ours, it's like "iron sharpening iron." God uses other people to rub our rough places smooth. This process is absolutely vital because only smooth stones will find their mark in the giant's forehead.

I would also like to apply this phrase, "and the rough places smooth," to the role our corporate worship fulfills in bringing us to Glory. The overarching goal of corporate worship is that we might be ushered together into the very Glory of God. In order to get there, however, the "rough places" must be made "smooth." What does that mean for us?

To answer that question, I want to refer to the occasion when David brought the ark of the covenant from the house of Abinadab (2 Samuel 6). Here's the heart of the story:

> So they set the ark of God on a new cart, and brought it out of the house of Abinadab, which was on the hill; and Uzzah and Ahio, the sons of Abinadab, drove the new cart. And they brought it out of the house of Abinadab, which was on the hill, accompanying the ark of God; and Ahio went before the ark. Then David and all the house of Israel played music before the LORD on all kinds of instruments of fir wood, on harps, on stringed instruments, on tambourines, on sistrums, and on cymbals. And when they came to Nachon's threshing floor, Uzzah put out his hand to the ark of God and took hold of it, for the oxen stumbled. Then the anger of the LORD was aroused against Uzzah, and God struck him there for his error; and he died there by the ark of God (2 Samuel 6:3-7).

The ark represents the Presence of God. David did not consult God as to the due order of transporting the ark, so God's anger was felt. David learned that you can't bring the Presence (ark) on a cart and expect Glory.

The cart represents man's tendency to automate the pathway to Glory. We try to "power" our services through to Glory. So we turn up the microphones, accelerate the tempo, sing the song one key higher, get everybody clapping and shouting at the same time, and consider that this is the way to attain Glory.

What is smooth to us is rough to God.

The cart seemed smooth to David because it was easy, but it was bumpy to God. The rickety ride over stones and knolls caused the ark to be jostled in the cart. In contemporary vernacular, I could imagine God saying, "Don't jerk Me around like this."

God's due order prescribed that the ark be transported on the shoulders of the priests. Now to the priests, that would seem to be the bumpy route to take. The priests would feel every bump in the road as they walked it one step at a time. But God would say, "No. This way may seem bumpy to you, but it's smooth to Me."

The same dynamic still happens in our worship services today. What is smooth for us is bumpy for God; and what is smooth for God is bumpy for us. Many of our "smooth" services coast quietly right past the Holy Spirit—a common syndrome which God defines as "rough." And then those "bumpy" times, when we don't know what God is doing, when we're crying out to Him for direction and help, when we're desperately longing for Him because His Presence seems distant—God says, "Now *this* is smooth! This is how I like it, when you're wobbly in your uncertainty and desperation, and clinging to Me with holy desperation."

Twice in the verses above it says that the ark was being transported from Abinadab's house "which was on the hill." In other words, the cart was on a downhill descent. Not only did the wheels help to mobilize the ark, but the incline caused the cart to move forward quickly. But the Lord was not impressed with the acceleration and momentum of the gathering. This illustrates a powerful truth for us: We must not confuse crowd momentum with Holy Spirit activity. Some of our services have a lot of outward dynamics at work with very few inner workings of the Spirit actually taking place. When we move too fast, we become presumptuous.

> ## We must not confuse crowd momentum with Holy Spirit activity.

It can be easy for worship leaders to become satisfied when they've been able to mobilize the congregation in a concerted expression of enthusiasm and clamorous praise, but then lack the discernment to perceive the lack of spiritual depth undergirding the surface activity. In times like these, it is tempting to mistake ministry momentum for God's endorsement.

God is making the rough places smooth by inverting our values, by drying up our satisfaction with "smooth services," and by reducing us to a desperate cry for kingdom reality— authentic manifestions of His power and Glory. The clinging desperation and trembling uncertainty feels bumpy to us but it's smooth to God.

And why is God exalting the valleys, leveling the mountains, straightening the crooked, and smoothing the rough? It's all in order that, "The glory of the LORD shall be revealed." There is nothing that heaven or earth or hell can do to stop it. God's Glory *shall* be revealed in the earth!

Isaiah goes on to say that when this Glory comes, "All flesh shall see it together; for the mouth of the LORD has spoken." Stay with me please, and before this book is through we will return to this truth, for one of the most powerful aspects of the coming Glory is the fact that *"all flesh shall see it together."*

When Presence Is Not Enough

*I*t is quite common to hear the words "Glory" and "Presence" interchangeably. Whether talking about the Glory of God or the Presence of God, we've meant basically the same thing. But they're not synonymous terms. In this chapter I want to walk you through the passage in which God helped me to see very clearly the distinction between these two powerful realities.

To understand the story in 1 Samuel 4 to which I want to take you, we need to agree on one simple interpretational equivalent: The ark of the covenant in the Old Testament represented the Presence of God. The ark was where God resided. The Lord said to Moses, "'I will speak with you from above the mercy seat, from between the two cherubim which are on the ark of the Testimony'" (Exodus 25:22). When God spoke to Moses, His voice proceeded from the empty space that was overshadowed by the wings of the cherubim, immediately above the mercy seat. Moses could point His finger into that area of thin air and say, "God is right *there* because I can hear His voice coming from that spot." So the ark was properly understood to be the seat of His Presence.

The ark was located in the Holy of Holies, the innermost sanctuary of Moses' tabernacle, which was separated from the Holy Place by a dividing veil. The ark was the only piece of furniture behind the veil. The ark was so closely associated with the Presence of God that the writer of Hebrews literally called the ark "the Presence" when he wrote, "This hope we have as an anchor of the soul, both sure and steadfast, and which enters the Presence behind the veil" (Hebrews 6:19).

So when you think "ark," think "Presence." That simple interpretive tool will unfold a passage which we are about to look at together. We're going to look at a story in which the people of God had the ark (the Presence) in their midst, but the ark was not sufficient to deliver them from their enemies.

The truth that I am about to share in this chapter was actually the catalyst for this book. One day as I was in the secret place and meditating in the story of 1 Samuel 4, the Lord opened a truth to my heart that continues to develop and grow within me. This story chronicles the time when the ark was captured by the Philistines, after which Eli's daughter-in-law uttered those classic words, "'The glory has departed from Israel!'"

You're welcome to read the entirety of 1 Samuel 4 right now, but for the purposes of our study together we will look at the story in sections. Here we go with the first four verses.

BRAINSTORMING SESSION

> *And the word of Samuel came to all Israel. Now Israel went out to battle against the Philistines, and encamped beside Ebenezer; and the Philistines encamped in Aphek. Then the Philistines put themselves in battle array against Israel. And when they joined battle, Israel was defeated by the Philistines, who killed about four thousand men of the army in the field. And when the people had come into the camp, the elders of Israel said, "Why has the LORD defeated us today before the Philistines? Let us bring the ark of the covenant of the LORD from Shiloh to us, that when it comes among us it may save us from the hand of our enemies." So the people sent to Shiloh, that they might bring from there the ark of the covenant of the LORD of hosts, who dwells between the cherubim. And the two sons of Eli, Hophni and Phinehas, were there with the ark of the covenant of God* (1 Samuel 4:1-4).

Our story begins in the context of a defeat. Israel had just lost a battle to the Philistines, four thousand warriors were dead, and now they were trying to figure out why God had not blessed their efforts and why they had lost.

The word of the Lord was with Samuel, but the nation was not ready to follow the spiritual leadership of this young prophet. The nation was being led by a collegiate group of elders (its first problem) instead of by the man with the word of the Lord. In the moment of crisis, the committee lacked the necessary discernment to find God's heart and chart the right course. They asked the right question: "'Why has the LORD defeated us today before the Philistines?'" But then they came up with the wrong solution: "'Let us bring the ark of the covenant of the LORD from Shiloh to us, that when it comes among us it may save us from the hand of our enemies.'"

> ### Instead of talking to God, they talked to each other.

Instead of talking to God, they talked to each other. I can imagine the elders holding a brainstorming session to figure out their next move. The moderator asked, "What shall we do?" Some said this; some said that.

Then one of the elders piped up, "Hey guys, listen, I have an idea! Remember the time when Joshua took the ark to Jericho, they carried the ark to battle, and then they gave a shout and the walls collapsed? How about if we were to try that? Maybe if we took the ark to battle, God would give us victory over our enemies, too."

Somebody responded, "That's a great idea! There is no way we can take the Presence into the battle and lose. By taking the ark to the battle, we're taking God with us! Having God with us in the battle is a sure guarantee that we won't be defeated."

Somebody made a motion, "I move that we reconnoiter, pull our army back together, bring the ark from Shiloh, let the priests carry the ark into the battle with us, and let's go forth and crush the Philistines!"

Somebody else said, "I second that motion."

The moderator asked, "Any discussion?" They threw it around for a while, fine-tuned the strategy, and then they called for the question. "All in favor say, 'Aye.'"

"Aye" said the chorus of voices.

"All those against say, 'Nay.'"

Silence.

"The motion is carried. Go and call for the ark. Gentlemen, we're going to war!"

DISCERNMENT

It's easy for us, with our objective perspective, to see what they did wrong. Instead of hearing from God and moving out in implicit obedience, they acted presumptuously according to their own creative thinking. "Ephraim is oppressed and broken in judgment, because he willingly walked by human precept" (Hosea 5:11). When we move out in the ingenuity of our own ideas, we forfeit the ability to exercise accurate judgment and discernment. And we meet up with the God who "makes the plans of the peoples of no effect" (Psalm 33:10).

Perhaps they were experiencing Job 12:20, "He...takes away the discernment of the elders." The unity of the Spirit is an essential element in helping elderships to move forward with God, and yet unity in and of itself is not always a guarantee of blessing. There is a time when the tyranny of consensus can blindside an eldership. It is a time when God tests an eldership by removing His counsel from the midst, to see if they will move ahead with human consensus when they have no word from God.

> *There is a time when the tyranny of consensus can blindside an eldership. It is a time when God tests an eldership by removing His counsel from the midst, to see if they will move ahead with human consensus when they have no word from God.*

Elders must always walk in brokenness before God, realizing the potential of unanimity without God's counsel is always there (1 Samuel 4:3). Elderships can be deceived into thinking that unanimity signals the mind of the Lord on a given matter. This is what happened to the Sanhedrin at Jesus' trial. Too easily elders gain comfort and confirmation in the false security of unanimous consensus. Most religious systems fall into decay under the guidance of the consensus of the elders. Elders need the voice of the prophets to save them at times from their own opinions. But in the case of our story, the elders didn't solicit the input of God's prophet, Samuel.

If we are to see God's Glory in this generation, it is crucial that the elders walk in godly discernment. I have been crying out to God, asking for the same thing that Paul prayed for the Philippians—"that your love may abound still more and more in knowledge and all discernment" (Philippians 1:9). Lord Jesus, I long for this discernment! (See Proverbs 2:3.) And I long for my brothers and sisters to grow in this spiritual discernment as well.

Discernment is the ability to distinguish between good and evil (Hebrews 5:14). True discernment is found through an abiding relationship with a Person—"The Spirit of wisdom and understanding" (Isaiah 11:2). Jesus connected discernment with understanding the times (Luke 12:54-59). I've been asking God to give me discernment of our times. I lack so much in this area. It seems to me, however, that we live in a "thorny" society. "'Now the ones that fell among thorns are those who, when they have heard, go out and are choked with cares, riches, and pleasures of life, and bring no fruit to maturity'" (Luke 8:14). The terrain of our times is a landscape of thorns. The cares of this life are literally choking the church, inhibiting her from pressing into God's Glory.

Virtually all pastors and worship leaders have experienced what it means to work real hard at planning the worship service, the songs and the music, only to get into the service and realize that God has decided to make their plans of no effect (Psalm 33:10). So what do we do now? God wants to train us in diligent listening, hearing His plans and purposes, and then walking in radical obedience and desperate dependence upon His leading.

In the story before us, the elders were in need of a spiritual breakthrough. They chose to bring the ark to the battlefront in the hopes that "'*it* may save us from the hand of our enemies'" (1 Samuel 4:3). They thought the power of deliverance was to be found in the ark itself. In other words, they had come to view the ark as a fetish, an amulet, a lucky charm that would, by virtue of its inherent power, give them victory over their enemies. Their lack of discernment was lamentable. Instead of consulting God, they reverted to experimentation. "Let's try it, see what happens." (Instead of being critical here, let's admit that most of us have also experimented when we needed a breakthrough.)

Here's what happened.

> *They had come to view the ark as a fetish, an amulet, a lucky charm that would, by virtue of its inherent power, give them victory over their enemies.*

THE ILL-FATED BATTLE

And when the ark of the covenant of the LORD came into the camp, all Israel shouted so loudly that the earth shook. Now when the Philistines heard the noise of the shout, they said, "What does the sound of this great shout in the camp of the Hebrews mean?" Then they understood that the ark of the LORD had come into the camp. So the Philistines were afraid, for they said, "God has come into the camp!" And they said, "Woe to us! For such a thing has never happened before. Woe to us! Who will deliver us from the hand of these mighty gods? These are the gods who struck the Egyptians with all the plagues in the wilderness. Be strong and conduct yourselves like men, you Philistines, that you do not become servants of the Hebrews, as they have been to you. Conduct yourselves like men, and fight!" So the Philistines fought, and Israel was defeated, and every man fled to his tent. There was a very great slaughter, and there fell of Israel thirty thousand foot soldiers (1 Samuel 4:5-10).

When the Philistines heard the shout of victory in the Israelite camp and discovered that the ark had come into the camp, they became desperate with fear. They rose up in a frantic sort of zeal and devastated the Israelite army. *This illustrates the reality that whenever we move forward into kingdom conquest, there is always a counter-attack, and we would do well to be prepared in advance for it.*

Now, here's what I saw as I read the story carefully. The people of God had the Presence of God (the ark), and they had the shout in the camp—and they lost the war! This contradicted everything I used to think about spiritual warfare. I used to think if we just got the Presence of God in the house and the shout of praise in the congregation, we would be guaranteed mighty exploits and great kingdom breakthroughs. But this account helped me to see something. The Presence wasn't enough! Even though they had the Presence and the victory shout, they still lost the war.

Here's the thought I'm submitting for your careful consideration: We need more than Presence. We need Glory. As we saw in this story, it's possible to have the Presence without the Glory. To complete the mandate of the Great Commission, we must see attention-grabbing, earth-shattering, hell-shaking, bondage-breaking demonstrations of the Glory of God.

Now let's finish the story.

THE GLORY IS DEPARTED

Also the ark of God was captured; and the two sons of Eli, Hophni and Phinehas, died. Then a man of Benjamin ran from the battle line the same day, and came to Shiloh with his clothes torn and dirt on his head. Now when he came, there was Eli, sitting on a seat by the wayside watching, for his heart trembled for the ark of God. And when the man came into the city and told it, all the city cried out. When Eli heard the noise of the outcry, he said, "What does the sound of this tumult mean?" And the man came quickly and told Eli. Eli was ninety-eight years old, and his eyes were so dim that he could not see. Then the man said to Eli, "I am he who came from the battle. And I fled today from the battle line." And he said, "What happened,

my son?" So the messenger answered and said, "Israel has fled
before the Philistines, and there has been a great slaughter among
the people. Also your two sons, Hophni and Phinehas, are dead;
and the ark of God has been captured." Then it happened, when
he made mention of the ark of God, that Eli fell off the seat
backward by the side of the gate; and his neck was broken and he
died, for the man was old and heavy. And he had judged Israel
forty years. Now his daughter-in-law, Phinehas' wife, was with
child, due to be delivered; and when she heard the news that the
ark of God was captured, and that her father-in-law and her
husband were dead, she bowed herself and gave birth, for her
labor pains came upon her. And about the time of her death the
women who stood by her said to her, "Do not fear, for you have
borne a son." But she did not answer, nor did she regard it. Then
she named the child Ichabod, saying, "The glory has departed
from Israel!" because the ark of God had been captured and
because of her father-in-law and her husband. And she said,
"The glory has departed from Israel, for the ark of God has been
captured" (1 Samuel 4:11-22).

When the Philistines captured the Presence (the ark),
Phinehas' wife said the Glory had departed. She was partly
right because the Glory of God had departed from Israel. But I
want to suggest the Glory didn't depart with the capture of the
ark. I want to suggest the Glory departed long before this story
ever took place. For many years now the nation had been without Glory, and all they had was Presence (the ark).

But now, even the Presence was gone! What a heart-wrench-
ing story! If you catch the passion of the moment you could
easily weep because the most precious possession of the entire
nation—the ark—had been captured. For seven months they
had no Presence. It was one of the lowest moments in the entire
history of God's people. Nothing could have been more devas-
tating to the morale of the nation. What dismay must have
gripped the hearts of the Israelites, who had convinced themselves the ark was unconquerable and they were invincible with
it. And now what was once thought impossible had actually
happened. The Presence was removed by the enemy. And they
had no idea if it would ever come back.

> ## *They thought they had Glory,*
> ## *but all they had was Presence.*

There was a time when they had not only Presence, they had Glory. The Glory of God resided upon the tabernacle in Moses' day. Moses had left a written record of how the Glory had descended at the dedication of the tabernacle. From the tabernacle's inception, it had been home to the cloud of Glory and the pillar of fire (Exodus 40:34-38). But over the course of the years, the Glory departed, and the people didn't even know it. Phinehas' wife thought that prior to the ark's capture they still had God's Glory upon the nation. They thought they had Glory, but all they had was Presence.

And Presence wasn't enough to win the war.

How the Glory Departs

 T o continue from the previous chapter, we said that in the context of the story of 1 Samuel 4, the Glory had departed long before the ark was captured. Over the years, the people had become accustomed to Presence without Glory and didn't even know what they were missing.

We know they lost Presence when the ark was captured by the Philistines. But when did they lose Glory? And how?

Well, we don't know exactly when the Glory departed from the temple. But this much is clear: *The Glory does not depart suddenly.* You don't have Glory one day and then not have it the next. Rarely is the exodus of Glory that clearcut and definitive. Usually it is a slower, degenerative process that happens over time.

EZEKIEL'S VISION

Ezekiel had visionary insight into this truth. God showed him that the Glory does not depart suddenly but gradually—in stages. It's a process. God revealed this truth to Ezekiel in a vision, showing to him the departure of the Glory from the temple. The Glory didn't just BOOM, depart. It moved progressively in a sequence whereby it rested at five different stations in its departure from the holy city. Each station represented a critical "point of decision," at which point the people needed to make spiritual choices. Either they would repent and turn, or they would continue on their downward spiral of compromise and wickedness. *Unchecked compromises among the people meant the Glory would progress to a more distant station in its departure from their midst.*

Station 1: When Ezekiel was first transported to the temple in his vision, he saw God's Glory. "And behold, the glory of the God of Israel was there, like the vision that I saw in the plain" (Ezekiel 8:4). Ezekiel noted that the Glory was in its place, in the Holy of Holies, above the ark's mercy seat and cherubim. "Now the glory of the God of Israel had gone up from the cherub, where it had been" (Ezekiel 9:3). So we start with the Glory in its rightful place, in the temple, with the cherubim, over the mercy seat, among God's people.

Corresponding compromise: The Glory was cohabiting, however, with "the seat of the image of jealousy" (Ezekiel 8:3) which was an image of Baal. The Lord gave them time to repent (see Revelation 2:21), but because of their refusal to repent the time came when the Glory began to depart.

Station 2: Because of their sinful compromise, the Glory moved to the threshold of the temple. "Now the glory of the God of Israel had gone up from the cherub, where it had been, to the threshold of the temple" (Ezekiel 9:3).

Corresponding compromise: Ezekiel was shown unclean beasts and idols portrayed on the walls, and he saw seventy elders offering incense to idols in one of the rooms of the temple's courts (Ezekiel 8:10-12). This represented another "point of decision," and because of their choices the Glory continued to depart.

Station 3: First Ezekiel saw cherubim that "were standing on the south side of the temple" (10:3). Then he said, "the glory of the LORD departed from the threshold of the temple and stood over the cherubim" (10:18). So now the Glory had moved from the threshold to the south end of the temple.

Corresponding compromise: Ezekiel saw women at the north gate of the temple, weeping for Tammuz (Ezekiel 8:14). The worship of Tammuz involved temple prostitution together with all its accompanying lewdness.

Station 4: The Glory moved with the cherubim and came to stand "at the door of the east gate of the LORD'S house" (10:19). The Glory was yet another step further from its rightful place.

Corresponding compromise: Ezekiel was shown twenty-five men who were in the inner court, worshiping the sun to-ward the east (Ezekiel 8:16). It's another point of decision, and because of the peoples' compromises the Glory made yet one more move.

Station 5: The Glory moved out of the city, to the mountain that is on the east side of the city. "And the glory of the LORD went up from the midst of the city and stood on the mountain, which is on the east side of the city" (11:23).

Corresponding compromise: Ezekiel sees twenty-five men at the East Gate, and they are devising iniquity and giving wicked counsel to the city (Ezekiel 11:1-2).

It is at this point the vision lifts. The last glimpse Ezekiel has of the Glory is as it stands on the mountain on the east side of the city. Where it went from there, he did not see.

Again, the point here is the Glory departs gradually, in stages, in response to specific compromises that are not renounced at critical points of decision.

SAMSON

The same truth is illustrated in Samson, who displayed an unusual dimension of Glory in his life through his superhuman strength. The Glory of God was manifest through him in a mighty way, but he allowed himself a series of compromises that eventuated in the Glory's departing from him.

Samson was a mightily anointed judge of Israel who was also a sucker for gratifying his natural passions. On one occasion, he indulged himself by sleeping with a harlot, and then he got up at midnight and carried the gates of the city to the top of a hill. He was mightily anointed and had powerful demonstrations of Glory through his life, but he was hazarding all that through his compromises.

Delilah, a beautiful Philistine woman, was an attraction for Samson that represented yet another in a string of compromises. But now his relationship with her was going to surface the true nature of Samson's deplorable spiritual condition.

His new love, Delilah, begged him to tell her the source of his strength. Under duress, Samson said to her, "'If they bind me with seven fresh bowstrings, not yet dried, then I shall become weak, and be like any other man'" (Judges 16:7). Samson didn't divulge the true secret of his strength, but he danced on the line of compromise. Delilah bound him with the fresh bowstrings in his sleep while men were lying in wait to apprehend Samson, but Samson "broke the bowstrings as a strand of yarn breaks when it touches fire" (Judges 16:9). What Samson did not realize is that the Glory was already moving toward the exit.

When Delilah accused him of mocking her, Samson said, "'If they bind me securely with new ropes that have never been used, then I shall become weak, and be like any other man'" (Judges 16:11). So Delilah bound him with new ropes during his sleep. Although Samson "broke them off his arms like a thread" when he awoke, he had failed at another critical point of decision. The Glory took another step away.

Once again Delilah whined that he had mocked her, so Samson said, "'If you weave the seven locks of my head into the web of the loom'" (Judges 16:13). This Delilah also did during his sleep, but Samson "pulled out the batten and the web from the loom" (Judges 16:14). And the Glory became even more distant.

After Delilah pestered and vexed him daily with her needling, Samson finally opened his heart to her and confided, "'No razor has ever come upon my head, for I have been a Nazirite to

God from my mother's womb. If I am shaven, then my strength will leave me, and I shall become weak, and be like any other man'" (Judges 16:17). Delilah lulled him to sleep and then had a man shave Samson's hair in his sleep. Delilah awakened him with the words, "'The Philistines are upon you, Samson!'" Samson said to himself, "'I will go out as before, at other times, and shake myself free!'" The next statement of Scripture is terrifying in its implications: "But he did not know that the LORD had departed from him" (Judges 16:20). He was as weak as any man, and the Philistines arrested, tortured, and maimed him.

> *His compromises had so desensitized him to the distancing of God's Glory that when the Glory finally left altogether he didn't even realize it!*

From Samson's perspective it seemed that the Glory left him suddenly, but in reality the Glory left him amidst a sequence of decisions, culminating in the total departure of the Glory from his life. His compromises had so desensitized him to the distancing of God's Glory that when the Glory finally left altogether he didn't even realize it!

WHEN THE GLORY DEPARTS FROM THE HOUSE OF WORSHIP

Now let's apply this truth to worship in the church. The church was created for Glory. Ideally, when the assembly of believers gathers to worship, the Glory should be present, igniting all the saints with holy fire. When Solomon gathered the nation together to worship at the newly constructed temple, and the singers and musicians "were as one, to make one sound to be heard in praising and thanking the LORD, and when they lifted up their voice with the trumpets and cymbals and instruments of music, and praised the LORD, saying: 'For He is good, for His mercy endures forever,' that the house, the house of the LORD, was filled with a cloud, so that the priests could not continue ministering because of the cloud; for the glory of the LORD filled the house of God" (2 Chronicles 5:13-14). The place of corporate worship was always destined by God to be the place of Glory.

Most denominations that exist today were birthed in Glory. When you read the histories of movements like the Methodists, the Salvation Army, the Assemblies Of God, the Foursquare Church, and many others, the common denominator in the inception of most church movements was an unusual degree of Glory manifest among God's people. In the earliest roots of most churches is Glory. However, for many the Glory has departed. The human syndrome of entropy seems to support this generalization: *The longer the existence of a certain church group or movement, the greater and more numerous are its opportunites to compromise and forfeit the Glory.* The wineskins of church structures, once flexible with the new wine of the fresh moving of the Spirit, always tend to calcify over time, hardening in their resistance to God's current intentions of Glory manifestations in the church.

> *If the Glory has never departed from your church, it's only because of one reason: You haven't been around long enough.*

I am not critical; I am merely being observant. How can any one of us be critical of the historic denominations, when the very factors that recurrently robbed them of the Glory over the centuries are also at work with every one of us—ever seeking to rob us of the Glory for which we were destined? If the Glory has never departed from your church, it's only because of one reason: You haven't been around long enough.

Virtually all church groups and movements that have known Glory have also known what it means for the Glory to recede and move toward the exit. This problem is universal and inevitable given enough time. The Glory recedes when we mismanage the critical decision points God places before us. So in our next chapter I want to continue this sequence of thought by looking at some of the wrong ways we tend to respond when we sense the Glory departing.

The Five Deadly D's When There's No Glory

Many of us have conceived of God's Presence as the ultimate attainment in our worship gatherings. We have thought that by having God's Presence in the midst of the community of faith we have uncovered New Testament Christianity. But I am saying God's Presence is not enough. It's possible to have His Presence without His pleasure (His smile). His Presence is great, but there's more. There's Glory. Most of us have known His Presence in our midst as we worship, but few of us have truly entered the Glory realm. *His Presence is His promise; His Glory is His pleasure.* We are assured the kiss of His Presence but not necessarily the smile of His Glory. The Glory realm is somewhat elusive. We desire it but rarely seem to experience it. And yet it's the fullness Jesus died to grant us.

Most Christian churches throughout the world experience the Presence of God (to some degree) when they gather together for corporate worship. God's Presence may not be discernable at the outset of the meeting, but as the incense of worship begins to arise, an awareness of God begins to grow in the room. As the hearts of God's people begin to lift in faith and praise, the gentle Presence of God begins to distill quietly in the room as He inhabits the praises of His people (Psalm 22:3).

POINT OF DECISION

However, it's precisely at this point that something critical often begins to happen. Although we sense God's Presence, we also sense a certain lack of fullness. We know we haven't experienced the breakthrough in the Spirit that we desire. We know we are in the Presence of Immanuel ("God With Us") and yet we know there's more. While the atmosphere is sweet, there's a clear awareness that we have not yet touched the Glory realm. Here's the distinction: *We have Presence, but not Glory.*

This syndrome has been experienced in virtually every Christian church around the world, in all generations. It's absolutely universal. I am emphasizing that point because I want you to understand that this chapter is in no way intended to poke at certain kinds of churches. I am not criticizing a certain style of worship, nor am I setting any one tribe of Israel (e.g. denomination) above another. Almost every single church has come to that point where they have Presence but not Glory. The only exception would be those churches which have not known even the Presence of God.

When we come to that place of having Presence without Glory, we have arrived at what I am calling "the point of decision." We are at a spiritual crossroads. How we respond to the Holy Spirit at this point of decision will determine our future destiny. The critical question is this: *What will you do when you have Presence but not Glory?* Your response will carry serious ramifications for the spiritual inheritance of your local church family.

> *The critical question is this:*
> *What will you do when you have*
> *Presence but not Glory?*

If you have ever been responsible for conducting a corporate worship service, then it's most likely that you can connect implicitly with what I'm saying. Chances are you know the feeling of being in front of the people, being in charge of the worship service, and having this lead-ball feeling in the pit of your stomach because you realize the worship service is in serious trouble. There's no Glory and you know it. In some cases, there's not even Presence. There are few things more uncomfortable than being the leader of a worship service where there's no Glory and even the sense of Presence is questionable. You just want the platform to open and swallow you alive. *But what you do in that moment carries significant implications for the worship life of your church.*

FIVE COMMON RESPONSES

When our worship services have no Glory, there are at least five possible responses common to church leaders. As an alliterative device, these five all start with the letter "D."

1. Delight

It's a rare but yet sad fact that some churches respond to the absence of Glory with delight. They don't want Glory, and they're quite happy when it leaves them alone.

Some leaders have looked at other churches where small manifestations of Glory have erupted and have cynically discarded what they've observed as undesirable and distasteful. They've looked at Glory and decided they don't want it. Because Glory has a way of annihilating all decorum and protocol, it usually comes with great controversy and opposition. Tommy Tenney has pointed out that the Presence of God will enable our flesh, but Glory will disable our flesh. When Presence comes, we are strengthened and empowered; when Glory comes, priests are no longer able to stand and perform their duties (2 Chronicles 5:14). And when people start to collapse on the floor, many will judge the meetings as "indecent" or "out of order." The furor that attends Glory is too costly for some leaders, and they're quite delighted when this Glory leaves them alone.

> *When Presence comes, we are strengthened and empowered; when Glory comes, priests are no longer able to stand and perform their duties (2 Chronicles 5:14).*

The truth is God's Glory is disruptive. It's untamed, uncontrollable, unstoppable, and dangerously all-consuming. It destroys agendas, calendars, service orders, songlists, and carefully devised plans. It frustrates, exposes, confounds, and renders powerless the controlling mechanisms of church leaders. Glory is dangerous and revolutionary. It's explosive, undomesticated, volatile, divisive, and invasive. Glory smashes in like a tidal wave, washing away the safety nets and lines of familiarity that have helped us feel secure. The clock might help to establish when the meeting starts, but it's useless in determining when the meeting might stop. Buildings become overcrowded, restrooms can hardly be kept clean enough, children seem to be everywhere, critics abound, the neighbors complain, cars are parked sideways, businesses bawk, mayors try to mediate, and other pastors are secretly envious that it's not happening at their place.

And people will do the weirdest things in response to Glory. Some will shout; some will dance; some will weep; some will clap; some will fall to the ground; some will kneel; others will shake uncontrollably. They will make strange sounds and weird bodily movements. They will miss meals and keep strange hours. And they won't have the slightest reservation about telling every single soul they meet in the grocery store about all the unconventional things happening in the meetings.

"No," some will say, "We don't want that. If that's what Glory means, then we don't want it." The pricetag is too steep. They refuse to relinquish control. The Lord never imposes Glory on those who don't desire it, and they're just as happy that that's so.

2. Despair
Now here's the other end of the spectrum. While some are delighted that Glory hasn't touched them, others are despairing because they're convinced they'll never see Glory in their lifetime. Some churches have given up. They no longer contend for Glory. It's been so long since they've had Glory that no one can even remember it. They're only contending for Presence now; they've given up all hope of seeing Glory. In fact, there are some churches that have even given up on Presence.

Some churches are profoundly grateful if they can have just a dusting of Presence. They go through their typical program (a.k.a. rut), and the entire time the worship leader is silently begging God for a breakthrough, "Please, please, please, please, please, please, please, please, please, please!" Every once in a while something will begin to stir. About 25 minutes into the service a faint breeze will gently begin to waft into the auditorium, and chins will be lifted slightly for just a moment as the hungry say, "Ah, what was that? Ah yes, I sense it now, there it is. It's the Presence of God."

And quickly, so as not to ruin the delightful effect of the moment with an anticlimactic nosedive, the leader steps in hastily to announce with great relief, "You may be seated." And all are satisfied that now we can move forward with the service order and then go out to eat, because we have once again tasted of the Presence.

> *Some churches are relieved when they're able to touch just a little bit of Presence; they've given up all hope of ever touching Glory.*

Some churches are relieved when they're able to touch just a little bit of Presence; they've given up all hope of ever touching Glory. Don't forget what we said earlier: You can have the Presence and the shout and still lose the war. God's Presence isn't enough. *Some churches have just enough Christianity to inoculate people against the real thing.*

Some groups no longer even expect or try to touch Glory. In despair, the leaders shrug and slip into a passivity that basically says, "There's nothing we can do about it. Live and let live." Other churches don't even have any Presence anymore. Their gatherings are so far from touching the Father's heart that they don't even expect or contend for Presence. It's been so long since God showed up, they've developed a ministry philosophy that doesn't even include the expectation to experience the Presence of God.

It's tempting for some to look down condescendingly upon churches that have lost the Glory and the Presence. But the truth is, if *your* church had been around as long as *their* church has been around, you would be struggling with the very same issues. These dynamics eventually affect every church, given enough time.

3. Default

With the first two categories of "Delight" and "Despair," chances are I didn't describe your church situation. But get ready, we're about to hit close to home. As you read the next three categories, it might be helpful if you let your first response be laughter. Laugh first, then you can weep.

What do you do when you've got Presence but not Glory? Some are delighted; others are despairing. Now here's our third response: Some hit the Default Button. Let me explain.

You get into the worship service, and you realize it isn't going in the right direction. It's obvious the congregation has not yet touched the heart of the Father and has not caught any upward surges of the Spirit's winds. Something is clearly wrong, but you have no idea what it is, and you don't know what to do about it.

In that moment of pain and uncertainty, many leaders hit the default button (to use computer language). There is a default button many leaders will revert to when they don't know what else to do. "When you don't know what to do, hit the default." What is this default button? It's simply this: *Go to the next song.* We default to the next thing in the service order. When you don't know what to do (so goes this logic), *sing another song.* You have enough experience in this thing to know good and well that the solution to a floundering service is not always the right song, but you're willing to give it another try anyways.

> *When you don't know what to do*
> *(so goes this logic), sing another song.*

Like the Israelite elders in the battle with the Philistines, you start to experiment. You go "fishing" for the right song. "Maybe this song will do it." "Well, that one didn't work, let's try this one." Now you can begin to feel the sweat running down your back. "Wow, this service is really in trouble. Let me see, let's try *this* song because it worked really great last week!"

Sometimes we relate to our songs like the elders related to the ark. We treat our songs like fetishes, like lucky charms that have power within themselves to effect change. *We default by pulling out another song, hoping that we'll hit upon the right song to "magically" pull the service out of its nosedive.* We ascribe to our songs a magical property they don't possess. For the Israelites the power to overcome was not in the piece of furniture called the ark, and the power to gain victory over the spiritual battles we encounter in worship services does not reside inherently within our songs. The ark was but a vehicle for releasing God's grace to His people—a vehicle which could be abused. Similarly, our songs are vehicles that God can use to dispense grace—"singing with grace in your hearts to the Lord" (Colossians 3:16). But they can also be abused when they are used in a way that is almost superstitious.

> *We treat our songs like fetishes, like lucky charms that have power within themselves to effect change.*

Many churches have developed what I would call a "song-dependent liturgy." (Although my upbringing and experience is primarily in Pentecostal and Charismatic traditions, what I am describing is not limited to those circles, this is relevant for virtually all denominations and streams.) I have been asking myself why so many churches depend so heavily on songs to unlock the spirit of worship they desire. Songs are powerful tools for releasing worship, but when we look to them in an imbalanced way, the Lord will sometimes cause them to be as powerless as the ark was for the Israelites on the battlefield. I love songs and singing, but the singing of songs is not the only way to worship. And songs are not the only means of grace God has given us to help touch His heart.

There are other "touchpoints of grace"—means whereby God's grace is released to us—besides the singing of songs.

Grace can also be released in our worship services through such things as the Eucharist, anointing with oil, washing of one another's feet, the laying on of hands, Scripture reading, agreeing prayer, prophetic utterances, giving, confession and repentance, altar response, exhortations, preaching, etc. In other words, our worship services are comprised of so much more than just songs.

When we are seeking to unlock Glory in our worship services, leaders will be more effective if they are released and empowered to lead in more than just songs. When worship leaders are limited to the singing of songs, they may be hindered from employing the means of grace intended by the Holy Spirit to unlock the atmosphere of the meeting. When a worship leader is released to do more than just sing songs, that leader will need to walk very closely with the pastor, and in the case of lesser experienced worship leaders, will need extra instructional input from the pastor. But really, aren't the risks worth it? Because what we cry for is Glory! We should not default to songs as though they can accomplish what only the Glory will accomplish. I would also add here that pastors should take a proactive role in standing alongside their worship leaders to contend for Glory together. The most effective leadership will be given when a team spirit of cooperative unity exists between the pastoral team and the worship leading team.

Instead of defaulting to another song, what would happen if the worship leader just STOPPED EVERYTHING and said, "We're missing it"? What would happen if we stopped and consulted God? "God, what is in Your heart in this moment? Your smile is obviously not upon our songs up to this point. How can we touch Your heart right now?" An inexperienced worship leader would need to be careful that he or she didn't employ this device as an escape from the weight of growing up into their responsibility before God and the people. But when a capable worship leader, with a contrite heart and a trembling spirit for God's Glory, is willing to get out of the rut of just singing another song, and take the risk of expressing his or her cry for God, I believe the Lord notices this kind of faith and passion.

What would happen if we stopped and consulted God?

"Wait a minute!" I can hear worship leaders remonstrating. "Are you suggesting, Bob, that as the worship leader I should stop right in the middle of the worship service, and confess that I don't know where the meeting is going? Isn't that vocational suicide? Surely you're not suggesting that we stop and consult God!"

I'm saying, "Why not?"

"No way! Not me! I'm not going to stick my neck out like that." After all, there are few things as intimidating as admitting before an entire congregation that you don't know where to go with the meeting. Such a posture makes us feel vulnerable, naked, inept, and out of control. In other words, it makes us feel like what we really are.

The alternative is to default. Just play it safe; sing the next song. Stay in the comfort zone. And miss the possibilities of touching the Father's heart and unlocking new dimensions of Glory.

4. Dial Up

This is a very common response of many worship leaders when they realize the gathering is not touching the Glory realm of God. They know something needs to change in order to have a breakthrough in the meeting, so they begin to "dial up" their intensity level. They revert to the arm of flesh and begin to stir the meeting up in their own strength.

"I can't hear you! Come on, people, lift your voices!"

Then, they give a signal to the musicians, "Give us a key change, one step higher." (A higher key will get everyone singing louder.)

"Let's all stand and praise the Lord! Don't let the rocks praise in your place!" (When people stand, it feels like they're more into it.)

"Everyone lift your hands!" (Now it really looks like something's happening.)

A little signal to the drummer: "Faster!"

"Put your hands together, let's make a clap offering."

"Be free. Dance before the Lord!"

A little thumbs-up to the lead guitarist means, "Turn it up a little bit."

Another signal to the dance and tambourine troupe gets them mobilized in the front altar area.

"If you've got the victory, then shout unto God with the voice of triumph!"

Faster, higher, louder, stronger, tighter. If God's not sending his Glory, well, we'll just do enough stuff to convince everybody that we've actually touched the Glory.

> *The efforts of worship leaders to produce a breakthrough are usually very sincere, but it's a common pitfall to mistake human activity for a spiritual breakthrough.*

The efforts of worship leaders to produce a breakthrough are usually very sincere, but it's a common pitfall to mistake human activity and participation for a spiritual breakthrough. *Just because everything is faster and higher and louder and more demonstrative does not necessarily mean that we've stepped closer to Glory.* In fact, it's possible for such efforts, when motivated from the flesh rather than the Spirit, to actually work against God's purposes for the gathering. Those with accurate discernment will realize the leader isn't moving in the Spirit, and they will sometimes find their soul resisting the leader's exhortations. When a resistant spirit grips a meeting, it's certain we're not going to touch Glory.

Many worship leaders get up-tight because of the resistance of the flock. Their exhortations to praise are tainted with a tinge of frustration. In my own personal history as a worship leader, there were times I got so mad at the people while leading worship that I could have kicked them. (They are called "sheep" you know, and sheep are stupid!) Inside I'm thinking, "I'm giving this service my best shot, and all you people can do is sit out there like a bunch of blobs and do nothing to stir up your soul and bless the Lord!" Some worship leaders, in their zeal for

God's house, have even slapped the bride with their words of frustration and anger.

> *Some worship leaders, in their zeal for God's house, have even slapped the bride with their words of frustration and anger.*

Before I move to the next point, I want to make an observation about something I've noticed in the church in this present hour. There are two basic elements to worship: initiation and response. In the present move of the Spirit, it seems to me in a general sense that the Spirit is honoring "response first, initiation second" (as opposed to initiation first, response second). Let me explain.

In initiation, we rise up in our souls to make His praise glorious, to praise Him with all our being according to the measure of His excellent greatness. It's our initiating toward Him. In response, we are being carried up on the impetus of the Holy Spirit and allowing Him to initiate toward us. As He initiates, we respond. Many worship leaders have a mental model of getting the people to initiate their praise, hoping that God will then come into the meeting and empower us to respond to His Presence. But the Lord is honoring the exact opposite. *He is honoring those leaders who are coming carefully into His Presence, waiting upon Him to initiate toward us, and then helping the people to respond back to the Lord with their reciprocating initiative.* In this model there is much less of a tendency toward hype because the Holy Spirit is seen as the one responsible for moving the people to worship—not the worship leader or musicians.

Thanks for taking that quick detour with me. Now back to the fifth way that we can respond when we are not seeing the Glory of God in our worship times.

5. Denial

We gather for worship, and about 25 minutes into it there comes a clear sense of connectedness in the Spirit, and the Presence of God begins to fall like dew in the room. There's a collective response as the congregation opens to the Presence of the

Lord. The worship leader is not just a little relieved. "Maybe they won't fire me after all," he muses. Everyone sits back for the sermon, satisfied that God is still in the midst.

"So what do you think?" we ask each other after the service. "Wasn't it good today?"

"Oh, yes!" comes the reply. "It was real good. What a worship service!"

"I mean, did we have church or what?!"

"Yessirree! We sure had church today!"

"And His Presence, wasn't it sweet?"

"Sweet? Yes, that's the word for it, it certainly was sweet today."

And nobody will admit that the Emperor has no clothes. Nobody will admit, "We have His Presence, but we don't have His Glory." We have the Presence and the shout, and we're losing the war. But we're all convincing each other that everything is as it should be.

> *Nobody will admit, "We have His Presence, but we don't have His Glory."*

Some of you reading this book are struggling right now in your attitudes toward your local church leadership, and you're thinking, "Boy, I wish my worship leader would read this and get the message!" Others of you are worship leaders, and you're thinking, "I wonder if people perceive me as in denial, or dialing it up."

I'm not writing this to fuel criticism or to surface insecurity in worship leaders. I'm writing this to be absolutely transparent about dynamics that are universal in the church but not always acknowledged. Don't let my words become ammunition for your discontentment. Rather, let's realize that we're all in this together because, I think I can safely say for most church leaders, we're all doing the best we know to do. When we struggle with our insecurities as leaders, or see the shortfall of others, we should commit ourselves anew to prayer. That's the direction I want this to point you—toward God—which leads to my final point.

DESPERATION: THE RIGHT RESPONSE

So what should we do when we have Presence but not Glory? If the answer is not Delight, nor Despair, nor Default, nor Dial Up, nor Denial, then what is the answer? In one word, it's "Desperation."

This is a response that says, "God, we don't know why we're not touching Your Glory, and we don't know what to do about it—but we're desperate for You!"

Desperate people will do anything to achieve their goal. They don't care about form, they don't care about public opinion, and they don't care about being in control or playing it safe. They're desperate!

Every church develops its own "groove" over time, a pattern or style of worship that becomes comfortably familiar to its congregation. Church members can almost predict precisely what's going to happen next because they've come to memorize the service order. This groove becomes a comfort zone, and anything that would push them out of that rut becomes a threat.

> *Desperate people no longer have regard for comfort zones.*

But desperate people no longer have regard for comfort zones. They don't care about maintaining the status quo because there's something they desire more than smooth services. *They have an insatiable cry for Glory!*

May the Lord put such a desperation in our hearts that would compel us to stop the "First Church groove," fall on our faces before God, and seek His Glory. When you don't know what's wrong with a given service, and you don't know what to do about it, try this: Consult God. Stop the machinery that so easily grinds its way right past the Holy Spirit, and let a desperate cry press you into the face of God. You might even say to the congregation, "Saints, I don't believe we have yet touched the heart of God in our worship service today. I don't know what to do, but I long to meet with God. Let's call upon the name of the Lord together!"

When we consider the possibility of stopping everything and consulting God, pastors and worship leaders must face some very difficult questions honestly:

- "Am I willing to hazard the awkwardness of admitting my poverty and wretchedness before the congregation?"
- "Am I willing to embrace uncertainty and tentativeness?"
- "Am I willing to lose control?"

This will require leaders to clothe themselves in humility and brokenness before the entire congregation, but if we've truly been made desperate by God, we won't care. Even if my uncertainty makes me appear foolish and inept, it doesn't matter because above all else I must see His Glory!

Unfortunately, many leaders and worship teams come to worship services to "do a job." Their job, as they see it, is to pull off a successful worship service, and they feel they've succeeded when the majority of the people leave the meeting with a sense of satisfaction and completion. This "job performance" mentality can potentially turn worship leaders into hirelings —leaders who are not giving their hearts in worship to God, but who are seeing to it that everyone else gives their love to God. This model of worship leading is no longer cutting it, it is not pleasing the Father.

> **Worship leading is "taking your private cry and making it public."**

Here's my definition of worship leading: Worship leading is "taking your private cry and making it public." It involves the vulnerability of taking your own personal yearning for God and expressing it to God in the presence of the entire congregation. Where are you really at before God in your personal walk with Him? Will you allow the people to see your own desperation for God? If you will come before the people in the authenticity of your own struggles and joys, and lift your heart to the Lord in simple transparency, I think you'll find that the congregation will eagerly follow you into the Presence of the King.

We haven't gathered to pull off a meeting; we've gathered to meet with God! Leaders who are desperate to see God will find the flock more than willing to follow them in that abandoned pursuit of His Glory.

Touching the Glory Realm

I am absolutely desperate to see God's Glory—and I believe you are too! One of the holiest hungers we can have is for the Glory of God. Oh to see His Glory! This was Moses' cry. He prayed, "'Please, show me Your glory'" (Exodus 33:18). The fact that God answered his prayer is proof that God is willing to hear and answer our cries for His Glory. Glory is coming, and it's something God wants *you* to touch.

In this chapter I want to begin to describe what this Glory looks like that we desire so earnestly, and how we can touch it. My goal is not simply to enlighten you to Glory's reality, but to ignite you with a fresh passion to see His Glory. My prayer is that as you read this chapter prayerfully, the Lord might stir your spirit deeply and awaken a renewed desire to behold His Glory.

When Moses prayed, "'Please, show me Your glory'" (Exodus 33:18), the backdrop to that prayer is strategically important. A number of significant events preceded this prayer which deserve our attention. Few men in the Bible had encounters with God's Glory like Moses did. It all began the day that Moses saw a bush that was burning in the wilderness but wasn't consumed.

You may be very familiar with Moses' story, but allow me to review his encounters with God's Glory and power:

- He saw a bush in the desert that was burning but not consumed. Then, he heard God's audible voice ordering him to take his shoes off because he was standing on holy ground. God proceeded to call him verbally to lead His people from Egypt to the promised land.

- He threw his rod down, and it became a serpent; then, he picked the serpent up by the tail, and it was a rod again.

- He put his hand into his bosom, pulled it out, and it was leprous; he returned his hand into his bosom, and when he withdrew it again, it was healthy.

- He watched as ten fearful plagues invaded Egypt: blood, frogs, lice, flies, pestilence, boils, hail, locusts, darkness, and death. These judgments of God exploded before Moses' eyes, reducing the nation of Egypt to ruination.

- A protective misty cloud clung breathlessly to the ground between Israel and Egypt's army while a fierce gale blew over the adjacent sea, dividing the waters.

- They walked through the sea, on dry ground, with a wall of water on this side and that.

- On the opposite shore they watched as the sea returned upon itself, killing Pharaoh's entire army. Corpses were strewn on the beach.

- The bitter waters of Marah were made potable by casting a tree into the waters.

- Manna from heaven appeared on the ground, and water poured forth from a rock when Moses struck it.

- Then, they came to the mountain where God Himself descended in fire and a thick cloud. Huge plumes of smoke billowed into the sky, there was lightning and thunder, the entire mountain shook, they heard a trumpet blast that kept increasing in volume, and then they heard the voice of God Himself. God warned on penalty of death lest any man or animal should venture onto the mountain. Then, He said to Moses, "Come on up!"

- Moses climbed the mountain at God's command and lived for two sets of forty days in the fire of God's Glory upon the mountain.

- Then, Moses asked to be shown God's Glory, and God showed him His back.

LEVELS OF SPIRITUAL INTENSITY

One of the first things you might notice about the above chronology is the general increase of intensity in Moses' encounters with God's Glory. The progression launches with his seeing a burning bush and culminates in his seeing God's back. This highlights the fact that there is a wide spectrum of intensity of spiritual realities— almost something akin to the way a volume control works on a radio. God can increase the intensity of His spiritual manifestations from virtual silence to deafening thunder.

There are varying degrees of intensity of Presence, and there are varying degrees of intensity of Glory. First, let's talk about the varying degrees of Presence.

> *There are varying degrees of intensity of Presence, and there are varying degrees of intensity of Glory.*

We realize that the Presence of Christ is manifest in varying degrees of intensity as we worship. At the most basic level, God is omnipresent (that is, He is everywhere at all times), and so He is always present with us. At a higher level, Jesus "presences" Himself when His people gather together in IIis name: "'For where two or three are gathered together in My name, I am there in the midst of them'" (Matthew 18:20). God's Presence is manifest even more clearly when His people praise and worship Him together: "But You are holy, enthroned in the praises of Israel" (Psalm 22:3). In other words, when we praise Him together, the Lord sits enthroned among His people. This dimension of His Presence is so palpable that we can often sense His Presence with us as we worship Him together. At times our awareness of His Presence during our corporate praise is very clear, and at other times it can become overpowering in its strength.

God has promised His Presence to us:

- "My Presence will go with you, and I will give you rest" (Exodus 33:14).
- "And lo, I am with you always, even to the end of the age" (Matthew 28:20).
- For He Himself has said, "I will never leave you nor forsake you" (Hebrews 13:5).

Whether our awareness of His Presence is weak or strong, we have the confidence that He is always with us. You might perceive that as both a threat and a promise, but the truth is that even though He is a consuming fire, we long for His Presence in our lives.

And even as there are degrees of intensity in the sphere of Presence, in a similar way there are degrees of intensity in the sphere of Glory.

THERE ARE DEGREES OF GLORY

This much is obvious: Moses did not experience the full dosage of God's Glory. If He had—there is no question about it—Moses would have died on the spot (see Exodus 33:20). God could only reveal to Moses a diluted or lesser degree of Glory. But even so, it was a greater manifestation of Glory than Moses had experienced up to that moment—even though he had been living in the fire for well over forty days.

The following diagram is my crude and inadequate attempt to try to illustrate the gradient intensities of God's personhood. Take it for what it's worth because this diagram only begins to portray the awesomeness of God's Presence and Glory.

I see Presence and Glory as comprising a continuum. Presence can become so strong that God crosses the divide and manifests His Glory in a tangible way. There is no end to the chart because the intensities of God's Glory are limitless. God's omnipresence (the level where 95% of earth lives most of the time)

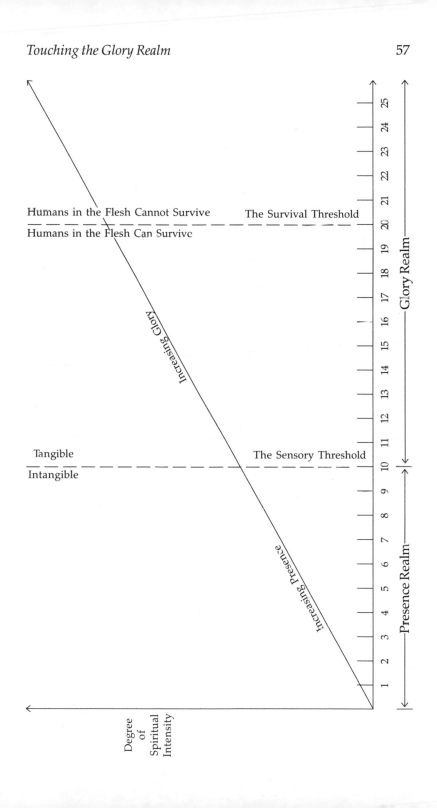

might register around a zero or a one in the Presence realm. His manifest Presence in a corporate time of high worship might register around a nine or a ten. And then we enter that sphere where we move from Presence to Glory—where we cross the sensory threshold. When God heals a sick person we're talking a Glory manifestation that might register around a twelve in the Glory realm. The survival threshold is that point where God's Glory becomes so intense that a person in this body of flesh would be killed if exposed to that level of Glory.

I really don't know how to write about or portray the varying degrees of Glory because it's a dimension that is for the most part beyond my personal experience to date. When I look at Psalm 19:1, I see it referring to the least level of Glory: "The heavens declare the glory of God." At this level, the Glory is not actually being experienced. By looking at the universe, the universe witnesses to the Glory of God. The universe cries out, "God exists, and His Glory is real." But that Glory is not experienced by looking at the heavens; it is only pointing to the existence of God's Glory.

> *God is preparing to bring us into a dimension of Glory that not even the living creatures in the throne of God can endure.*

The greatest intensity of Glory the Bible describes is recorded, in my opinion, in Revelation 15:8: "The temple was filled with smoke from the glory of God and from His power, and no one was able to enter the temple till the seven plagues of the seven angels were completed." This verse is not talking about Solomon's temple or any earthly temple; it's talking about the true temple in heaven. God's Glory filled the heavenly temple with such intensity that no one—no angel, no elder, no cherub, no living creature, no one—was able to enter that Glory. This intensity of Glory would be "off the chart" of our earlier diagram. It's amazing to consider that the holy ones who inhabit the very throne of God and who dwell among the fiery stones are not able to sustain the fullness of God's Glory when it is manifest! But the intimation of Scripture is that we, the church, are being prepared for this dimension of Glory. God is preparing to bring us into a dimension of Glory that not even the living creatures in the throne of God can endure. The Glory that awaits Jesus' bride is beyond all imagination! Saints, the witness of Scripture is true: We have no idea what God has prepared for us! Oh, but it certainly is glorious just to ponder these things.

BACK TO MOSES

Let's get back to Moses, on the mountain. This is one of the most sublime stories in the entire Bible. In obedience to God's call, Moses ascended the mountain into the thick darkness where God was, into the very fire of God. He was up there for forty days, neither eating nor drinking, at which time he received the Ten Commandments written on stone tablets.

He came down the mountain, saw the people worshiping a gold calf, smashed the stone tablets, destroyed the gold calf, and then went back up the mountain for a second set of forty days. He was a total of eighty days on the mountain! No food, no drink, just living in the immediacy of the fire of God's Presence. He didn't realize it, but He had been so irradiated by the fiery aura of God that his face was starting to shine with its own luminescent radiance. And it's here, during this second set of forty days on the mountain, he prayed his classic prayer, "Please, show me Your glory."

GOD'S RESPONSE

I would almost expect God to be angry at such a request. In my natural thinking I could imagine God saying, "After all you've seen, Moses, and after all the Glory I've shown you, all you can do is stick your boney little hand out there and ask for *more*??" But instead of being angry, God actually favored his request. Let's look at the story in Exodus 33, beginning with verse 12 (the verses are numbered for easy reference).

> 12 *Then Moses said to the LORD, "See, You say to me, 'Bring up this people.' But You have not let me know whom*

You will send with me. Yet You have said, 'I know you by name, and you have also found grace in My sight.' 13 Now therefore, I pray, if I have found grace in Your sight, show me now Your way, that I may know You and that I may find grace in Your sight. And consider that this nation is Your people." 14 And He said, "My Presence will go with you, and I will give you rest." 15 Then he said to Him, "If Your Presence does not go with us, do not bring us up from here. 16 For how then will it be known that Your people and I have found grace in Your sight, except You go with us? So we shall be separate, Your people and I, from all the people who are upon the face of the earth." 17 So the LORD said to Moses, "I will also do this thing that you have spoken; for you have found grace in My sight, and I know you by name." 18 And he said, "Please, show me Your glory." 19 Then He said, "I will make all My goodness pass before you, and I will proclaim the name of the LORD before you. I will be gracious to whom I will be gracious, and I will have compassion on whom I will have compassion." 20 But He said, "You cannot see My face; for no man shall see Me, and live." 21 And the LORD said, "Here is a place by Me, and you shall stand on the rock. 22 So it shall be, while My glory passes by, that I will put you in the cleft of the rock, and will cover you with My hand while I pass by. 23 Then I will take away My hand, and you shall see My back; but My face shall not be seen" (Exodus 33:12-23).

In verse 14, God said to Moses, "'My Presence will go with you.'" This was actually a change from God's position earlier in the chapter when God said that instead of accompanying them personally He would send an angel with them into Canaan. God's reasoning was, "'I will not go up in your midst, lest I consume you on the way, for you are a stiff-necked people'" (Exodus 33:3). God was wearying of the fact that every time He drew near to His people, thousands of them would die because of His holiness and their waywardness. But Moses pled with the Lord, so He changed His mind. God decided to accompany them personally. In verse 14, He assured Moses, "'My Presence will go with you.'"

Moses' reply in verse 15 was basically saying, "Oh good, Lord! Because if Your Presence doesn't go with us, we don't even want to go. I'm not even willing to lead this thing if You're not coming with us."

In verse 16, Moses makes the fascinating observation that the Presence of God is the distinguishing earmark of God's people. Our corporate gatherings have many of the same elements of worldly nightclubs and bars: good fellowship, great music, and even food and drink. But there's one thing we've got that they don't have, and that's the Presence of God! Without His Presence, we may as well close the doors and join the world. It's His Presence that separates us from all others.

> ### *The Presence of Christ in our congregations is an absolute guarantee.*

In verse 17, God seals His commitment with a second assurance. Basically God is saying, "Okay, Moses, you've got it. My Presence is guaranteed. It's a done deal. I will be with you." This wonderful assurance of God continues to us today. God still promises to be with us. He has said to us unequivocally, "'For where two or three are gathered together in My name, I am there in the midst of them'" (Matthew 18:20). The Presence of Christ in our congregations is an absolute guarantee. We don't have to sing in His Presence; we don't have to clap up or shout up His Presence; we don't have to pray down His Presence. When we gather in His name, His Presence is immediate and certain. Praise God, He is with us!

But now Moses responds to the Lord in verse 18, and I will paraphrase in an expanded way what I hear Moses saying. "Thank you, LORD, for Your Presence. Without your Presence, I resign. I'm so glad You're promising us Your Presence. We need it desperately! But..." (Moses pauses and hesitates) "...it's not enough. I want more. I want more than just Your Presence. I want Your Glory. Please, show me Your glory!"

The Lord revealed His delight in Moses' request by assenting. The Lord's response was like this, "Okay, Moses, in your case I'm going to say yes. Here's what I'm going to do. I will make all My goodness pass before you, and I will proclaim the name of the LORD before you. I will be gracious to whom I will be gracious, and I will have compassion on whom I will have compassion." God chose to give Moses one of the most unique revelations of Himself of any man in history (other than Jesus Himself).

WHAT EXACTLY IS THE GLORY?

The first question this account raises is this, "What is God's Glory?" When we ask to be shown His Glory, what are we asking for?

I believe the Lord Himself gave us a two-fold description of Glory in verse 19. The first aspect of Glory is found in His words, "'I will make all My goodness pass before you.'" God was essentially saying, "Moses, you're actually going to see something. You will see My Glory with your natural eyes." So the first dynamic of Glory is that it is perceived by one or more of the five senses, at the natural sensory level. It is an encounter where you literally see, hear, smell, taste, or actually feel spiritual realities. It's not the level of "inner impressions" but of actual physical experience. Some people have actually smelled a heavenly aroma during worship services. Others have seen a cloud or angels or even Jesus Himself. Others have heard angels singing or God speaking. When you have a spiritual experience that is actually perceived at the sensory/physical level, then you're touching the Glory realm. That's the first half of Glory.

> *The first half of Glory: We perceive spiritual realities with one or more of the five senses, at the natural sensory level.*

The second half of Glory is described in the Lord's next phrase of verse 19, "'And I will proclaim the name of the LORD before you.'" God was saying, "Moses, I am going to proclaim My name before you in such a way that it goes beyond a physical hearing and becomes a true spiritual hearing. I will cause My words to explode within your spirit. The Spirit of wisdom and revelation will ignite like a bomb within your heart and mind, the eyes of your understanding will be enlightened, you will actually comprehend the full portent of what I am speaking to you, and you will come to know Me better." This is God revealing God to the human spirit, and it doesn't get any better than this! This is the part of Glory that really excites me. It's not just a sensory experience, but it's also an experience whereby the Holy Spirit supernaturally enables us to comprehend spiritual truth in our inner man so that we might know Him better. Wow!

> *The second half of Glory: The Holy Spirit supernaturally enables us to comprehend spiritual truth in our inner man so that we might know Him better.*

This two-fold definition of Glory is consistent with the apostle John's experience (as well as many others in the Bible). As per his account in Revelation 1, John literally saw the risen Christ with his natural eyes, but the experience didn't stop there. Jesus then proclaimed His name to John: "'I am the Alpha and the Omega, the Beginning and the End, who is and who was and who is to come, the Almighty. I am He who lives, and was dead, and behold, I am alive forevermore. Amen. And I have the keys of Hades and of Death'" (Revelation 1:8, 18). John's heart must have nearly exploded with the revelational insight of Christ's words as He spoke these awesome truths straight into John's spirit. John not only saw and heard, he also understood. *This* is Glory!

Glory is the realm of the lifted veil (2 Corinthians 3:18)—when God lifts the veil that separates us from the eternal sphere and reveals to us spiritual realities. I have defined God's Glory as "the invasion of God's reality into the human sphere." God's Glory is very real, even more real than the physical universe, but we don't see it. But, occasionally, God will invade our physical sphere with His spiritual realities, and when that happens we taste of Glory.

HOW DO WE TOUCH THE GLORY REALM?

As I write about these things, I get holy heartburn. My heart starts to ache with anticipation and longing and desire. Perhaps, as you read, yours does, too. The question that naturally follows, then, is this: "How do I touch this Glory?"

We want it so badly, and we want to know how to experience it ourselves. We're not satisfied with reading of Moses' experience. We don't merely want to enjoy Glory vicariously through Moses. We want to experience Glory for ourselves! But what must we do to touch this Glory?

> *Glory is something for which you must contend.*

Moses' example teaches that you must *ask* for Glory. Glory is something for which you must *contend.* It doesn't just fall into your lap, you have to go after it. "'Please, show me Your glory.'"

But asking for Glory is no guarantee we'll fully experience what we desire. As God continues to speak of this in verse 19, He is actually revealing to us something about His ways. God said, "'I will be gracious to whom I will be gracious, and I will have compassion on whom I will have compassion.'"

In other words, God is saying, "I will bestow this grace upon whomever I choose to bestow it, whenever I decide to, in whatever manner I choose." He is telling us that the dispensing of Glory is administered entirely under the jurisdiction of His royal sovereignty. God gives Glory to whomever He decides, whenever He decides. It is guarded by His own sovereign choice. He gives it when He wants; He withholds it as He wants. It is all of mercy.

> *In other words, God is saying, "I will bestow this grace upon whomever I choose to bestow it, whenever I decide to, in whatever manner I choose."*

This gives me hope because God didn't reveal Glory to Moses based upon some arbitrary qualification that I'll never be able to meet. It wasn't because Moses was so old; or because he had white hair; or because he was so likeable; or because of his body weight. It had nothing to do with Moses' natural features or personal charisma. God simply decided, "In your case, Moses, I'm going to say yes." This gives me hope that he might choose to say yes to me, too.

All we can do is stand there, quivering with desire, and ask. Beg. Implore. Pant. Yearn. We have no control over whether or not He decides to show us His Glory. We can't fast and pray our way to Glory, or prophecy ourselves into Glory, or dance into the Glory, or give offerings that induce Glory, or shout down the Glory. (Mind you, most of us have given those things a good try.) We can't earn it, deserve it, or work it up. In Moses' case He said yes. In my case—well, all I know to do is ask. And keep asking. "Lord, have mercy on me, and show me Your Glory."

GOD UNFOLDS HIS STRATEGY

Now let's proceed with our story, how God revealed His Glory to Moses. God said, "'You cannot see My face; for no man shall see Me, and live.'" God knew that if Moses saw His face he'd suffer cardiac arrest on the spot. The human body can sustain only certain levels of Glory. So God made provision for Moses so that he would survive the encounter.

God decided to show Moses His back. However, if this wasn't done right, Moses would end up dead. I can imagine God saying, "Okay, Moses, I'm going to show you My back. But I want you to cooperate with me in this thing because, if we don't do this right, you'll fry.

"Tell you what I'm going to do, Moses. I'm going to place you in this cleft in the rock, so that there will be a wall of rock between you and My face. But if all you have is this wall of rock between you and My face, you'll still fry. So I'm going to give you double protection. I'm going to give you the wall of rock, and I'm also going to cover you with My hand.

"Then I'm going to walk past the outcropping of rock. When I move past the protective rock, Moses, then I'm going to take My hand away as well, and you will have a direct, unfiltered, unveiled view of My back. And then I will proclaim My name to you."

Okay, that's the plan. We understand. All right, Moses, finish the chapter. Now to verse 24. Tell us what happened next.

There...is...no...verse...24. What?? Moses! Don't stop there. Finish the chapter!! Don't do this to us, Moses! We want to know, *what happened??* What was it like? What did you see? What did you feel? What happened inside of you when He proclaimed His name to your heart?

MOSES IS MUM

It's as though Moses is saying, "I'm not talking about it. There are some things that are inexpressible beyond words. You just can't talk about them."

But if Moses were to tell us about what happened, I think we might be surprised at his tale. When God removed His hand, I think Moses was totally unprepared for the intensity of what flashed before him. I can imagine Moses saying, "I can't talk about it. Words can't begin to describe it. He moved past the rock, so that the rock was no longer between Him and me. And then He removed His hand. And I looked, and..." WHOOOOOOOOOOOOSHH!!

My personal opinion is that the encounter nearly killed him. If seeing the face of God would have killed him, I'm suggesting that seeing the back of God nearly killed him. It was as much Glory as any one human in the flesh could possibly sustain without dying. Since coming within a hair of one's death is not generally considered a delightful proposition, I am suggesting that the encounter was not altogether pleasant for Moses. It may have taken him days to recover. (Note Daniel 8:27.)

> *If seeing the face of God would have killed him, I'm suggesting that seeing the back of God nearly killed him.*

And now here we are, looking the pricetag square in the face, and lining up to say, "Us too, Lord! Show us Your glory!"

You might think we're a little demented or deranged. Who in their right mind would ask to be nearly killed?

I realize I don't know even know what I'm asking when I say it, but I'm saying it anyways. "Lord, show me Your glory! I've got to see You, and I'm desperate to hear You proclaim Your name to my heart. Me too, Lord!"

TWO INCREDIBLE VERSES

When I consider the intensity of Moses' experience with Glory, there are two verses in the Bible that totally amaze me. The first is written by Moses, the second by Paul.

The first verse I'm referring to is spoken by Moses right at the end of his life. He said to the Lord, "'You have begun to show Your servant Your greatness and Your mighty hand'" (Deuteronomy 3:24). Moses was essentially saying, "Lord, I have seen Your Glory in some very strong ways. I have seen Your fire; I have lived for weeks in the flame of Your holy mountain; and I have beheld Your back. But I recognize that it's really been only the beginning. I have only *begun* to see Your greatness. The intensity of Glory that awaits me in the eternal city is beyond anything I can even begin to imagine."

Wow! What might that Glory be like? One day we will know.

The second verse that amazes me is written by Paul in his second letter to the Corinthians. He devoted the third chapter of this epistle to the topic of Glory. As he wrote of the Glory that Moses experienced and how it even caused his face to radiate light, Paul then compared that Glory to the Glory of the New Covenant. And here's how he described the comparison: "For even what was made glorious had no glory in this respect, because of the glory that excels" (2 Corinthians 3:10). Under the inspiration of the Holy Spirit, Paul was saying that when we compare the Glory Moses experienced under the Old Covenant with the Glory we have entered into with the New Covenant, the Glory that Moses knew will be considered "no glory."

Heaven's Glory will be so intense
that we will look back on what
Moses experienced and call it "no Glory."

We are headed for such magnificent Glory, beloved, that when we look from the Glory of heaven at the Glory Moses experienced, we will not merely call it "lesser Glory." Nor will we call it "little Glory." In truth, we will call it "no Glory!" We will perceive what Moses tasted as such insignificant Glory as to be considered non-existent. Here's my question: Lord, what kind of Glory have you prepared for us, that once we have experienced it we will consider Moses' view of Your back as having no Glory at all in comparison?

SUBJECTIVE PRESENCE VS. OBJECTIVE GLORY

We won't know fullness of Glory until the next life, but there are degrees of Glory that God sometimes grants in this life. Let's contend for these manifestations of Glory! Oh Lord, please show us Your Glory, and proclaim Your name to our spiritual minds!

I am speaking of the *objective* Glory of God. Presence is subjective, Glory is objective. Let me explain.

Have you ever come out of a worship service and had the person sitting next to you walk out lit up like a lightbulb? They're saying, "Wow, was that awesome! God sure was in the house today! That's the best service we've had in this place in a long time!" And they're walking on six inches of air.

But you look at them like they're from a different planet. Because as far as you were concerned, that was one of the deadest services you've ever been in. That kind of thing happens a lot, doesn't it. For them, the service was incredibly rich; for you, the service was dry and lifeless. I call this "the Presence realm."

In the Presence realm what various people experience becomes a very subjective, individualized thing. One person receives one thing, another person feels something totally different. One person is superblessed, another feels totally bypassed; one person is blitzed, another person is falling asleep. When God visits us with His Presence, everyone responds or receives differently based upon their faith level, intensity of concentration, and how God chooses to touch them in the uniqueness of their own personal challenges and needs.

But the Glory realm is objective. By "objective" I mean that everybody experiences the same thing in the same way because God has moved past spiritual impressions into physical manifestations. The Glory realm was what happened when the cloud filled Solomon's temple during its dedication ceremonies (2 Chronicles 5). *Everyone* saw the cloud; *none* of the priests were able to stand to perform their service. The Glory became an objective reality in the physical realm.

> ## When Glory comes, "all flesh shall see it together."

On the mount of transfiguration, Peter didn't say to James and John, "Hey guys, can either of you see Moses? Can you see Elijah? Does anybody else see the cloud? Maybe I'm just having a trance." No, they all saw Moses and Elijah, they all saw Jesus in His Glory, they all saw the cloud, and they all heard the voice of the Father. They all experienced the same thing; it was Glory.

On the Day of Pentecost, everyone in the group of 120 heard the sound of a mighty rushing wind, they all had tongues of fire settle upon them, and every one of them spoke in other languages. Everyone saw and experienced the same dimensions of Glory.

When Glory comes, "all flesh shall see it together" (Isaiah 40:5). The critics will be silenced; skeptics will be dumbfounded; agnostics will believe; atheists will tremble; the sinners in Zion will be terrified; the righteous will rejoice; backsliders will repent; the indifferent will be shaken; the hot will be set to boiling; the cold will be forced to a decision; children will be set ablaze; the elderly will be revitalized; the hardened will be judged; the harvest will be gathered; the Father will be glorified. Men will experience together irrefutable manifestations of God's reality, and everyone will be forced to admit, "Truly God is among them." I am describing GLORY!

GLORY IN THE CHURCH

Listen, beloved: The church was birthed in Glory! Right from the beginning at Acts 2, God breathed Glory into the DNA of what our corporate identity is all about. We were created for Glory (Isaiah 43:7). You've been promised Presence, but Glory is in your genetics. You'll always be grateful for Presence, but you'll never be satisfied until you touch Glory.

> *You'll always be grateful for Presence, but you'll never be satisfied until you touch Glory.*

And let me tell you how this Glory is going to be manifest. There is only one medium for God's Glory in the earth. It won't land in the ocean or hit the middle of some continent somewhere. This Glory of which we speak is destined to come *through the Church*. This is what Malachi foretold, "And the Lord, whom you seek, will suddenly come *to His temple*" (Malachi 3:1). Haggai 2:7-9 and many other Scriptures make a clear connection between Glory and the temple. Paul reinforced that truth when he wrote, "To Him be glory *in the church* by Christ Jesus to all generations, forever and ever. Amen" (Ephesians 3:21). This is what the church has been panting for, and I'm writing this book to trumpet this as clearly as I can: IT'S COMING!

Oh my, and when it comes! God can accomplish more in one outpouring of Glory than our combined labors can produce in ten years. Oh, let a holy desperation grip your soul. There's more! Lord, please show us Your Glory!

Show Me *Your* Glory

*T*he focus of this book is primarily on the manifestation of God's Glory through the worshiping church of Jesus Christ. We want demonstrations of Glory in our corporate gatherings! However, there is another aspect to Glory that is precious and exciting, and it has to do with God's Glory coming privately to an individual.

In fact, that's the context for the central verse of this book. Moses prayed, "'Please, show me Your glory'" (Exodus 33:18). He didn't pray, "Show *us* Your glory." He prayed, "Show *me* Your glory." Moses was asking for a personal encounter with God's Glory, and God gave it to Him.

You've gotten this far in this book for only one reason: You have an insatiable cry for God's Glory. We are peering into His Glory because we are trembling with longing, filled with the passionate cry of David, "Oh, when will You come to me?" (Psalm 101:2). God brings His Glory to congregations, but He also visits individuals with Glory. "Yes, Lord! Me too!"

> *There are some things I can do to prepare myself personally for a private visitation of Glory.*

One reason this simple truth is so strongly encouraging to me is because, when I look at the greater body of Christ, I sometimes question how much work God might have to do before He's ready to release His Glory in the church. God forbid I should die before we see His Glory; I want a share of the action! It makes me feel helpless because there's comparatively little that I can do individually to prepare the global church for Glory. However, there are some things I can do to prepare myself personally for a private visitation of Glory. So this gives me the hope that if I'm diligent and faithful before God, I might at least be favored with a personal encounter with His Glory, even if the larger body of Christ isn't ready yet.

TWO KINDS OF GLORY BREAKTHROUGH

I see two general ways in which God crosses the cosmic chasm and touches us with His Glory. Firstly, He sends His Glory from heaven to earth. It is for this which Isaiah cries, "Oh, that You would rend the heavens! That You would come down!" (Isaiah 64:1). Revelation 8:5 is a graphic description of God's doing just that: "Then the angel took the censer, filled it with fire from the altar, and threw it to the earth. And there were noises, thunderings, lightnings, and an earthquake."

When God rends the heavens in his manner, it is sometimes to visit His corporate church with Glory. This is what happened on the Day of Pentecost, Acts 2:1-4, when the sound of a mighty rushing wind filled the room and tongues of fire came to rest on each one of them. This is God's reality invading the human sphere, appearing to entire groups of people and transforming entire cities. These kinds of Glory manifestations are increasing as we approach the return of Christ. However, when God rends the skies and comes down, it is not always for a corporate gathering; sometimes God rends the heavens to visit an individual (e.g. Job).

So God may come down and visit you personally with Glory. But it's not the only way He can do this thing. It's possible that He may also open a door in heaven and take you up to Glory. That's the second Glory breakthrough! There were several in the Bible who experienced this dimension of Glory, but in every case their encounter with Glory was exclusively a personal one. They were caught up to heaven alone; no one else accompanied them. It was solely an individual encounter with Glory. The Bible never records an entire group being caught up into heaven, only individuals, one at a time. And God is still meeting with certain individuals in the same way in these last days.

Following are just a few scriptural examples of private encounters with Glory:

- Isaiah saw the Son seated on the throne in heaven: "In the year that King Uzziah died, I saw the Lord sitting on a throne, high and lifted up, and the train of His robe filled the temple" (Isaiah 6:1).
- Daniel was caught up to heaven and chronicled his experiences. "I watched till thrones were put in place, and the Ancient of Days was seated; His garment was white as snow, and the hair of His head was like pure wool. His throne was a fiery flame, its wheels a burning fire" (Daniel 7:9).
- Paul writes rather cryptically about his own similar experience. "I know a man in Christ who fourteen years ago—whether in the body I do not know, or whether out of the body I do not know, God knows—such a one was caught up to the third heaven" (2 Corinthians 12:2).
- The apostle John also described what happened to him. "After these things I looked, and behold, a door standing open in heaven. And the first voice which I heard was like a trumpet speaking with me, saying, 'Come up here, and I will show you things which must take place after this'" (Revelation 4:1)
- Ezekiel had a number of experiences that were similar in nature. He wrote, "So the Spirit lifted me up and took me away" (Ezekiel 3:14). "He stretched out the form of a hand, and took me by a lock of my hair; and the Spirit lifted me up between earth and heaven" (Ezekiel 8:3).

Lord, I don't care if You choose to rend the heavens and come down, or if you open the heavens and take me up. Either way is fine by me; the only thing I ask is that I might behold Your Glory!

I think it's normal and healthy for Christians to look at experiences like these and to pant for their own similar encounter with God's Glory. It is my personal perspective, as I mention elsewhere in this book, that there is nothing we can do to guarantee ourselves a visitation of Glory. The only thing I know to do is what Moses did. Moses just asked. So just ask Him. "Please, show me Your glory."

However, it is also my personal perspective that there were two dynamics in Moses' life that qualified and prepared him for his stunning encounter with Glory. First of all, he was shown God's Glory in the context of 80 days of fasting and isolation on the mountain. This reflected an exceptionally unusual degree of consecration on Moses' part. Not very many people are willing to get away from everyone and be with God, alone, for such extended periods of time—and with no food or drink! My personal opinion is that Moses' intense consecration to God was a prime contributing factor to His being shown such Glory.

There was yet another element that in my opinion was a factor for God's showing Moses His Glory. It had to do with Moses' years of waiting for the fulfillment of God's promises. I am referring to Moses' forty years of preparation in the Midianite desert. While still in Pharaoh's house, Moses was called of God to deliver the people of Israel. His mistake was that he tried to fulfill a godly vision with human strength. In his natural zeal, he killed an Egyptian who was beating on a Hebrew slave, and thus he became hunted by Pharaoh. Moses had to flee Egypt, and he ended up in the Midianite wilderness where he lived for forty years. He eventually died to any desire or expectation of leading God's people to freedom. Moses' wilderness was a place of breaking and re-shaping into a new vessel that would be useful to God.

> *When I study the lives of those*
> *who had profound personal encounters*
> *with God's Glory, almost all of them*
> *had a common denominator in their history:*
> *a protracted season of waiting on God*
> *before the visitation of Glory.*

WAITING ON GOD

When I study the lives of those who had profound personal encounters with God's Glory, almost all of them had a common denominator in their history: a protracted season of waiting on God before the visitation of Glory. Invariably the waiting period included a fiery ordeal of testing, the postponement and even seeming annulment of divine promises, and painful personal restrictions of various sorts. Generally (but not as a hard and fast rule), the more intense the crucible, the shorter the duration.

Some of you have been waiting on God for a long time now, even for many years. You carry a promise in your spirit but have yet to see the fulfillment of God's deliverance. When you've been waiting on God for a period of years, it becomes necessary to focus your best energies on keeping your hope and confidence firm. The nature of the enemy's warfare in your life is to cause you to become discouraged and to cast away your confidence. Not that you would necessarily discard your salvation, but you could give up your hope of God's deliverance. The enemy wants to numb you into a coping kind of Christianity that has given up hope of seeing God's resurrection power.

> *The longer God's promise was delayed,*
> *the more Abraham's faith grew.*

The Scripture makes a fascinating statement about the 25-year period during which Abraham waited for the fulfillment of His promise: "He did not waver at the promise of God through unbelief, but was strengthened in faith, giving glory to God" (Romans 4:20). God promised him a miracle boy, and he waited 25 years for the fulfillment of that promise. Romans 4:20 describes that 25-year period of waiting. It says that Abraham's faith was stronger at the end of the 25 years than at the beginning. In other words, the longer God's promise was delayed, the more Abraham's faith grew. This is absolutely un-humanlike! Our human tendency is to believe that the longer a promise remains unfulfilled, the chances of the promise coming to pass are diminished with every passing moment. But the Abraham-kind-of-faith grows during the season of waiting because it is daily strengthening itself in God's word.

One reason many who have waited on God have given up is because they have not understood the duration of the crucible. They have not been able to see any redemptive value in the length of the wait, so they've concluded that they're simply incapable of touching God's heart in the matter. However, God sees great value in lengthy waits. He will purposely design waiting periods of multiple years for His chosen ones. And the overarching reason is because He is preparing them for a visitation of Glory. Those who wait with "faith and patience" are candidates for inheriting great promises (Hebrews 6:12).

> *He will purposely design waiting periods of multiple years for His chosen ones. And the overarching reason is because He is preparing them for a visitation of Glory.*

It's one thing to wait for a few years; it's quite another thing to wait for forty years! God made Moses wait for forty years in the wilderness before He appeared to him in the burning bush. Forty—count them—years! Initially I really struggled with this. I said, "Lord, that's *mean!* Making the guy wait that long... Don't even talk to me about forty years, Lord! I don't want to hear so much as a whisper about forty years. In forty years I'll be dead and buried!"

So I had a real hard time understanding why a God of compassion and mercy would make a guy like Moses wait for forty interminable years. But then God reminded me of the Glory Moses experienced—the burning bush, the Egyptian plagues, the Red Sea divided, 80 days on the mountain in the fire. And of course the capstone—Moses saw the very back of God.

Then, it was as though the Spirit of God whispered this question to my heart, "Was all that Glory worth forty years?" The inference was that the intensity of Glory Moses experienced was directly proportional to the length of the preparation period. The longer the wait, the greater the Glory.

If you're not presently in a crucible of waiting on God, these thoughts could possibly strike you as morbid. You would not find this to be a very joyful gospel. However, if you've been waiting on God for many years and have fought to maintain clarity and perspective on the ordeal, these words are probably greatly encouraging. Is it possible, dear waiting saint, that the reason for the extended trial is because of the Glory God has destined to pour upon your life? Could it be that the fiery wait is in fact a kindness? Could it be that God has a Glory invasion with your name on it? This is the hope I am convinced is affirmed over and over in the Scriptures.

> *Is it possible, dear waiting saint,*
> *that the reason for the extended trial*
> *is because of the Glory God has*
> *destined to pour upon your life?*

THE APOSTLE JOHN

This principle is affirmed so frequently in the Bible that I'm a little torn to figure out just which other example to use here. Well, let's look at the beloved apostle, John. (I look at other examples in my book *The Fire Of Delayed Answers.*) John was called the disciple whom Jesus loved, and the fact remains that those He likes most are often called upon to wait the most. Since He targets His chosen ones with Glory, He also targets them with a corresponding crucible to prepare them for that Glory. For John, the crucible was being exiled on the island of Patmos. He wrote:

> *I, John, both your brother and companion in the tribula-*
> *tion and kingdom and patience of Jesus Christ, was on the*
> *island that is called Patmos for the word of God and for the*
> *testimony of Jesus Christ. I was in the Spirit on the Lord's*
> *Day, and I heard behind me a loud voice, as of a trumpet, say-*
> *ing, "I am the Alpha and the Omega, the First and the Last,"*
> *and, "What you see, write in a book and send it to the seven*
> *churches which are in Asia: to Ephesus, to Smyrna, to Pergamos,*
> *to Thyatira, to Sardis, to Philadelphia, and to Laodicea"* (Rev-
> elation 1:9-11).

Scholars estimate that John was around 90 years of age at
the time of this experience, give or take a couple years. So he's
right at the end of his life, and here he gets exiled to the island of
Patmos because of his faith.

I can imagine John thinking, "Not now, Lord! I'm too old for
this. Not only do I not have the physical stamina for this, I don't
have the time either. I'm ready to die any moment, and this isn't
exactly the way I was expecting to go out. With all the maturity
and grace that You have invested in my life, surely You have
more fruitful things for my closing days of ministry than to have
me rot on this desolate island!"

But despite his old age, John responded to the imprison-
ment with the "patience of Jesus Christ," and instead of having
a grumpy attitude he devoted himself to be "in the Spirit." He
set his love upon his Lord despite his personal pain level. And
because he waited patiently on God and stayed in the Spirit, he
was granted the greatest revelation of Jesus Christ ever given
to a human being on earth. My, what Glory he suddenly beheld!
The heavens were opened, and He saw God. And then Jesus
opened His mouth and proclaimed His name to John. It doesn't
get any better than Jesus declaring Jesus to the human spirit!
This is Glory!

John waited patiently for Glory; let's wait for Him as well.

THE PREPARATION PROCESS

When God destines to manifest His Glory to an individual,
He always prepares that vessel through an individualized pro-

cess of character formation. Valleys are filled in, mountains are brought down, the crooked places are straightened, and the rough places made smooth (see Chapter Three). Our responses to God's testings determine whether or not we will see the end intended by the Lord. "You have heard of the perseverance of Job and seen the end intended by the Lord—that the Lord is very compassionate and merciful" (James 5:11). Because he endured the test, Job was rewarded with a visitation of Glory. God pulled back the curtain and revealed Himself to Job in a whirlwind. Not only did Job see God, he also heard God's voice as God revealed Himself powerfully to Job's heart through the Spirit of wisdom and revelation. Job received a thrilling encounter with God because he persevered.

The pathway to Glory is described masterfully by Paul:

> *Therefore, having been justified by faith, we have peace with God through our Lord Jesus Christ, through whom also we have access by faith into this grace in which we stand, and rejoice in hope of the glory of God. And not only that, but we also glory in tribulations, knowing that tribulation produces perseverance; and perseverance, character; and character, hope. Now hope does not disappoint, because the love of God has been poured out in our hearts by the Holy Spirit who was given to us* (Romans 5:1-5).

At the conclusion of this passage Paul has us looking to the hope of Glory, but let's work our way through the passage to see how we get there.

In verse 3, Paul says we can "glory in tribulations" because we understand what they produce in our lives. I consider this to be one of the greatest challenges of Christian maturity, to get to the place where we actually rejoice and glory in great tribulations. We will arrive at the place of rejoicing in tribulations sooner once we fully know that our tribulations are moving us toward Glory. The sheer magnitude of this Glory causes us to view the tribulations as our friends, for they have been the catalyst for this awesome Glory.

Then Paul delineates the process. It starts with this truth, "tribulation produces perseverance." Now, "tribulation" is just a fancy word for "pain." Pain produces perseverance. I know this truth well because for years I felt like my entire existence was nothing but pain and perseverance, pain and perseverance. One foot in front of the other. Month in, month out. I couldn't understand why it hurt so much and why God wasn't giving me light. For three dark years my life was described by those words, pain and perseverance. Now to verse 4.

Paul continues, "And perseverance [produces] character" (verse 4). When you persevere in the face of Christ through the pain, this kind of holy perseverance produces character. Another word for character is "Christlikeness." This character or Christlikeness is the true gold we buy in the fire (Revelation 3:18). When you persevere through the fire and the pain, you are changed more and more into the image of Jesus. I remember the day when it was as though I awakened from a dream, I pinched myself to be sure I was really awake and realized, "I'm different! I'm changed!" Suddenly I was able to see that the greatest crisis of my life was being used by God for redemptive purposes, to transform me into the image of Christ.

The passages goes on, "And character [produces] hope" (verse 4). When you see God producing godly character in you through the fiery trial, hope springs to life in your heart. It's the hope of Philippians 1:6, that the God who started this good work in you is going to complete it. When God starts into you, He doesn't get bored and move on. Nor does He throw up His hands in exasperation and say, "You're hopeless!" No, when He starts something, He finishes it. He is both the Author and the Finisher of your faith.

Verse 5 continues by saying, "Now hope does not disappoint." In other words, this hope is not an ethereal, wispy, vaporous kind of hope that rises up one moment and is gone the next. No, this hope has come through the fire; it's come through the flood; it's come through the waters; it's come through the darkness; it has survived the fury of the storm. This hope is hardened, durable, and strong. When you buy this kind of gold in the fire, you don't sell it, squander it, trade it, lose it, neglect it, or abandon it. No, what you buy in the fire is yours to keep. This gold is Christlikeness, it's eternal treasure, and it's yours forever. The hope that has survived this fire will never disappoint because it has proven the love of God in the greatest valleys of life.

> *When you see God using your pain to make you more like Jesus, a hope begins to grow within your soul that He is preparing you for a personal encounter with His Glory.*

But once you've come through this fire, what is the object of this hope? What are you hoping for? The answer is found back in verse 2, "We...rejoice in hope of the glory of God." The hope that fills your heart is this: God has been bringing you through such great tribulation because He is preparing you for great Glory! When you see God using your pain to make you more like Jesus, a hope begins to grow within your soul that He is preparing you for a personal encounter with His Glory. You gain more and more confidence that God's Glory will be known in you and through you, both in this life and in the life to come. Hope is the buoyancy of spirit that enables us to endure until the Glory has come.

I have written this chapter aware that some readers have been waiting on God and persevering through great pain and unfulfilled hopes. Take heart! As you persevere, you will be changed into the likeness of Christ Himself. And when you see that happening, hope will fill your heart because you know He will finish the good work, and will bring you unto Glory.

"And now, Lord, what do I wait for?" (Psalm 39:7).

I wait for this hope of Glory!

"O God, I don't care if You rend the heavens and come down, or open a door in heaven and take me up-but I've got to see Your Glory! This is everything I'm waiting for, everything I'm persevering for, everything I'm longing for. For this hope I will wait on You, I will guard my purity, I will deny myself, I will be faithful in good works, and I will abide in Your word. I will do *anything* to see Your Glory! Show me the beauty of Your face; proclaim Your name by the spirit of wisdom and revelation to my heart. I've simply got to know You! If You don't show me Your Glory, I think I'm going to die. Oh, when will You come to me? Do not turn away my tears, do not turn a deaf ear to my cry. Please, show me Your glory."

Today Is the Day!

Glory is coming! God is about to visit His people and it is our duty to be ready, alert, discerning the signs, waiting.

We live in a strategic hour. Having stepped into the third millenium, there is a sense of anticipation throughout the body of Christ. Things are brewing in the Spirit. Dedicated houses of prayer are springing up everywhere, venting the desperation of our hearts for a Glory breakthrough. Thunderclouds of holy invasion are boiling on the horizon. Great expectation is filling the hearts of the watchful.

> *Thunderclouds of holy invasion are boiling on the horizon.*

THE THIRD DAY

We have just stepped into the third millenium since Christ's coming. Understanding "that with the Lord one day is as a thousand years, and a thousand years as one day" (2 Peter 3:8), we have now entered "the Third Day" of church history—that is, the third period of one thousand years.

I believe that Jesus will return on the Third Day—within the next one thousand years. Even as Jesus graced the wedding in

Cana on the third day (John 2:1), so He will host the wedding supper of the Lamb on the Third Day of New Testament history. And even as He rose from the grave on the third day, the Lamb's wife will be resurrected into her glorified state on the Third Day. "After two days He will revive us; on the third day He will raise us up, that we may live in His sight" (Hosea 6:2). Jesus said, "'Destroy this temple, and in three days I will raise it up'" (John 2:19), which actually becomes a prediction that Jesus will raise up His true temple, the church, "in three days"—that is, in the third millenium after His earthly ministry.

You may be thinking, "Big deal! So what if Jesus comes back 935 years from now? That doesn't empower me to live with any great sense of anticipation for the here and now."

Yes, but consider this: Jesus rose from the dead *early* on the third day! Since Jesus' resurrection was in the beginning moments of the third day, "while it was still dark" (John 20:1), it becomes very reasonable to believe that He will also resurrect His bride *early* on the Third Day!

Furthermore, powerful manifestations of Glory will invade this planet prior to His return. In other words, Glory is about to invade Earth in unprecedented ways in this, the final Day of history. "This is the Day the LORD has made; we will rejoice and be glad in it" (Psalm 118:24). Get ready to rejoice, His Glory is coming! "'Surely it is coming, and it shall be done,' says the Lord GOD. 'This is the Day of which I have spoken'" (Ezekiel 39:8).

PREPARING FOR THE THIRD DAY

I want to close this book by looking at one final portion of Scripture, a passage that relates the coming Glory to the Third Day. Notice the references to "the third day" in these verses.

> *And the LORD said to Moses, "Behold, I come to you in the thick cloud, that the people may hear when I speak with you, and believe you forever." So Moses told the words of the people to the LORD. Then the LORD said to Moses, "Go to the people and consecrate them today and tomorrow, and let them wash their clothes. And let them be ready for the third day. For on the*

third day the LORD will come down upon Mount Sinai in the sight of all the people. You shall set bounds for the people all around, saying, 'Take heed to yourselves that you do not go up to the mountain or touch its base. Whoever touches the mountain shall surely be put to death. Not a hand shall touch him, but he shall surely be stoned or shot with an arrow; whether man or beast, he shall not live.' When the trumpet sounds long, they shall come near the mountain." So Moses went down from the mountain to the people and sanctified the people, and they washed their clothes. And he said to the people, "Be ready for the third day; do not come near your wives." Then it came to pass on the third day, in the morning, that there were thunderings and lightnings, and a thick cloud on the mountain; and the sound of the trumpet was very loud, so that all the people who were in the camp trembled. And Moses brought the people out of the camp to meet with God, and they stood at the foot of the mountain. Now Mount Sinai was completely in smoke, because the LORD descended upon it in fire. Its smoke ascended like the smoke of a furnace, and the whole mountain quaked greatly. And when the blast of the trumpet sounded long and became louder and louder, Moses spoke, and God answered him by voice (Exodus 19:9-19).

God instructed Moses to prepare the people because on the third day He was going to visit them with Glory. So the people sanctified themselves, spouses withheld from marital relations, and they washed their clothes.

And then early on the third day, "in the morning" (verse 16), the people awoke to God's Glory on the mountain. Their senses were assaulted with manifestations of Glory. First of all, they *saw* Glory—lightnings, a thick cloud, smoke, and fire. Secondly, they *heard* Glory—thunderings, a loud trumpet, and then the voice of God Himself. Thirdly, they *felt* Glory—the whole mountain shook and quaked.

What an awesome and terrifying encounter with Glory this was! God spoke to them in their own Hebrew tongue, enunciating what we call "the Ten Commandments" (Exodus 20). "And so terrifying was the sight that Moses said, 'I am exceedingly afraid and trembling'" (Hebrews 12:21).

Since we are now living in the Third Day, that makes the Third Day our *Today*. Our Today is the last Day of church history.

"Today, if you will hear His voice: 'Do not harden your hearts, as in the rebellion, as in the day of trial in the wilderness'" (Psalm 95:7-8). "But exhort one another daily, while it is called 'Today,' lest any of you be hardened through the deceitfulness of sin" (Hebrews 3:13). God's Glory is coming—Today!

> *Since we are now living in the Third Day, that makes the Third Day our* **Today.** *The Holy Spirit is saying, "Get ready, sanctify yourselves, for* **Today** *I am coming to you in Glory."*

The Holy Spirit is saying, "Get ready, sanctify yourselves, for *Today* I am coming to you in Glory."

This is why we are embracing fasted lifestyles; this is why we are seeking to consecrate more and more of our hearts to the Lord; this is why we are devoted to radical obedience; this is why 24/7 worship and intercession is springing up around the globe (24 hours a day, seven days a week of non-stop corporate prayer). We know that Glory is coming, and we're preparing ourselves because the Third Day has become Today.

EARMARKS OF THE COMING GLORY

I believe we will see intensifying manifestations of Glory as Christ's return approaches, even as Moses' experiences with Glory increased in intensity. His encounters with Glory began at the level of a burning bush and a rod turned into a serpent. Then they escalated to the intensity of ten destructive plagues in the nation of Egypt. But even more intense was the parting of the Red Sea and the drowning of Pharoah's army. Heavier still was the manifestation of God's Glory on Mt. Sinai, and His voice speaking audibly to the entire nation. From there, Moses ascended the mountain and lived within the fire for 80 days without food or drink. And finally, he saw the back of God. His experiences with Glory were progressively greater and greater until the zenith—he saw God Himself. In the same way, our experiences with Glory will be increasing in the last days until that time when we see Him face to face.

Beloved, I am writing to you about more than just fanciful ideas or wistful dreams. It is absolutely going to happen. God's Glory is going to visit His church in ever-increasing spheres, and the impact of the explosion will be felt to the four corners of the earth. The earmarks of this Glory visitation will include:

- Saints set ablaze with zeal for the face of Christ.
- A sharp increase of persecution and martyrdom.
- An explosion of miracles, signs, and wonders.
- A massive ingathering of souls.
- The catastrophic endtime judgments of God, as per Revelation 16, with devastation in the earth and men raging against God.
- Purity and fear in the church.
- The hardening of the pseudo-church (i.e., false religious systems).

This Glory is coming! Hear the word of the Lord: "The Lord *will* give grace and glory" (Psalm 84:11). The determined God has vowed, "'And I *will* fill this temple with glory'" (Haggai 2:7). "'But truly, as I live, all the earth *shall* be filled with the glory of the LORD'" (Numbers 14:21).

And when this Glory comes, it will not come as a little drizzle or misting that will touch a few here, and a few there. No! Hear how the word of God describes this coming Glory invasion: "For the earth will be filled with the knowledge of the glory of the LORD, *as the waters cover the sea*" (Habakkuk 2:14). The Holy Spirit is not describing a sprinkling, but rather a total immersion. This coming Glory will flood the entire earth with a *deluge* of power and divine determination.

> *This coming Glory will flood the entire earth with a **deluge** of power and divine determination.*

Oh my soul, my soul! When I think about these things my heart burns within me. I look around at what is, and I get very unsettled. I become agitated in my spirit. I am not at rest; my soul begins to churn within me, I become distraught and a little bit cranky. And I begin to think, "What's wrong with me? Why am I so discontented with business-as-usual? Others seem to be happy enough. Others seem to be content with the Presence realm as we've known it. Is it right for me to feel this way? What is this longing that burns within me? I am so satisfied with the sweetness of Jesus, and yet I am so dissatisfied. What's wrong with me? What is this?"

And then the Lord gave me a Bible word for it. It's called *lovesickness* (Song of Solomon 2:5; 5:8). I love Him so much, I am sick with love. I am sick because my love has not been requited with fullness. I am sick with love because He has still withheld Himself from me. I have seen enough of Him to be chronically addicted to His beauty, and I must know Him better. I am a Jesus junky. I'm ruined—for Glory! How can I ever be satisfied with anything less?

And so I stand trembling on the threshold of the Third Day, yearning, longing, weeping, begging. I can't live without You, Lord. I must see You! I must hear Your voice! Come to me, O my Beloved, lest I die! Show me Your glory!

"Oh, when will You come to me?" (Psalm 101:2).

"The Holy Spirit says: 'Today'" (Hebrews 3:7).

Amen!

Description of Resources on the Facing Page

❖ SECRETS OF THE SECRET PLACE—Bob shares some of the secrets he's learned in making the secret place energizing and delightful. Gain fresh fuel for your secret devotional life with God! (to be released in 2001)

❖ PAIN, PERPLEXITY & PROMOTION looks at the book of Job from a fresh, prophetic vantage. Job's life shows how God promotes His chosen vessels to higher heights then they would have conceived possible. Let Job's example compel you toward God's highest and best!

❖ THE FIRE OF GOD'S LOVE compels us toward the passionate love that God is producing within the bride in this hour for her Bridegroom, the Lord Jesus.

❖ THE FIRE OF DELAYED ANSWERS explores how God sometimes delays the answers to our prayers in order to produce godly character in us. This book is "spiritual food" for those in crisis or difficulty.

❖ IN HIS FACE propels the reader passionately toward a more personal and intimate relationship with Jesus Christ. Challenging devotional reading.

❖ EXPLORING WORSHIP is a 300-page textbook that covers a full range of subjects related to praise and worship. Translated into several languages, this best-selling book is being used internationally as a text by many Bible colleges, Bible study groups, and worship leading teams. Also available is an accompanying WORKBOOK/DISCUSSION GUIDE.

❖ DEALING WITH THE REJECTION AND PRAISE OF MAN is a booklet that shows how to hold your heart before God in a way that pleases Him in the midst of both rejection and praise from people.

Order Form

Books by Bob Sorge

	Qty.	Price	Total
BOOKS:			
SECRETS OF THE SECRET PLACE	____	$12.00	____
GLORY: When Heaven Invades Earth	____	$ 8.00	____
PAIN, PERPLEXITY & PROMOTION	____	$12.00	____
THE FIRE OF GOD'S LOVE	____	$12.00	____
THE FIRE OF DELAYED ANSWERS	____	$12.00	____
IN HIS FACE: A Prophetic Call to RenewedFocus	____	$11.00	____
EXPLORING WORSHIP: A Practical Guide to Praise and Worship	____	$13.00	____
Exploring Worship WORKBOOK & DISCUSSION GUIDE	____	$ 5.00	____
DEALING WITH THE REJECTION AND PRAISE OF MAN	____	$ 8.00	____

SPECIAL PACKET #2

	Qty.	Price	Total
One of each book	____	$65.00	____
(Special Packet Includes Free Shipping)			

Subtotal	____
Shipping, Add 10% (Minimum of $2.00)	____
Total Enclosed	____

U.S. Funds Only

Send payment with order to: Oasis House
P.O. Box 127
Greenwood, MO 64034-0127

Name _____

Address: Street _____

City _____ State _____

Zip _____

For MasterCard/VISA orders and quantity discounts,
call 816-623-9050

Or order on our fully secure website:
www.oasishouse.net